LIVING COMPASSION

LOVING LIKE JESUS

ANDREW DREITCER

UPPER
ROOM BOOKS®
NASHVILLE

Upper Room Books® website: books.upperroom.org

Upper Room®, Upper Room Books®, and design logos are trademarks owned by The Upper Room®, Nashville, Tennessee. All rights reserved.

Scripture quotations not otherwise noted are from the New Revised Standard Version Bible, copyright 1989 National Council of the Churches of Christ in the United States of America. Used by permission. All rights reserved.

Scripture quotations marked AP are the author's paraphrase.

At the time of publication all websites referenced in this book were valid. However, due to the fluid nature of the Internet, some addresses may have changed or the content may no longer be relevant.

Cover design: Jeff Miller | Faceout Studio
Interior design: Kristen Goble | PerfecType

Library of Congress Cataloging-in-Publication Data

Names: Dreitcer, Andrew, 1957- author.
Title: Living compassion : loving like Jesus / Andrew Dreitcer.
Description: Nashville : Upper Room Books, 2017. | Includes bibliographical references. |
Identifiers: LCCN 2016056670 (print) | LCCN 2017039659 (ebook) | ISBN 9780835817240 (mobi) | ISBN 9780835817257 (epub) | ISBN 9780835817233 (print)
Subjects: LCSH: Compassion—Religious aspects—Christianity. | Love—Religious aspects—Christianity. | Jesus Christ—Example.
Classification: LCC BV4647.S9 (ebook) | LCC BV4647.S9 D74 2017 (print) | DDC 241/.4--dc23
LC record available at https://lccn.loc.gov/2016056670

To Issy, Steffani, Hannah, and Monica:
Thank you for
showing me
the meanings of Love.

CONTENTS

ACKNOWLEDGMENTS

Every idea, every image, every aspiration expressed in this book carries the imprint of individuals and communities who have molded the perceptions, beliefs, emotions, understandings, and commitments of my life. While it's not possible to list all those who have played such roles, I'm very grateful to have the opportunity to acknowledge those who have most fully influenced what I offer in these pages.

The Compassion Practice that lies at the heart of this book derives from the spiritual practice and genius of my friend Frank Rogers. Frank, our friend Mark Yaconelli, and I spent a number of years shaping and reshaping Frank's core practice—until it took the form found here. More than anyone else, Frank and Mark have directly influenced the contents of *Living Compassion*. Without them, the Practice, the book, and my present understanding of compassion would not exist.

In addition to my work with Mark and Frank, interactions with many other people have helped me engage explorations of compassion in my (continuing) hope that I might become more and more informed, open, curious, and wise.

My teachers Henri Nouwen, Margaret Farley, Hans Frei, David Kesley, Sandra Scheiders, Eric Dean, and Raymond Williams impressed upon me the vital connection between the spiritual life and compassion-based scholarship.

Isabel Deeter Lewis, Ware Wimberly, Bill and Tracy Wimberly, John Schule, Ben Campbell Johnson, Elizabeth Liebert, and Howard Rice mentored me in the ways of a spirituality that is practical, effective, societally transformative, infused with humor, and deeply attentive to the realities of daily life.

Certain communities of faith have deeply shaped my life. The brothers of the Taizé Community, during the year I spent there, grounded

7

me in the ways of contemplative practice. Sleepy Hollow Presbyterian Church allowed me to bring contemplative practices into the life of a local congregation. Imani Community Church comforts and inspires me, challenging me to live into a spirituality that seeks peace with justice in the face of racial and cultural inequities.

Conversations with Betsy Deeter, Kay Collette, Tish Bulkley, Michael Spezio, Alane Daugherty, Cliff Saron, Rick Hanson, David Addiss, and students and colleagues at Claremont School of Theology have deeply formed and informed my spiritual path, my research, and my teaching.

Jeffrey Kuan, Sheryl-Kujawa Holbrook, faculty colleagues, and the Board of Trustees of Claremont School of Theology generously supported the writing of this book by granting me a research leave.

Doug Hagler, Jeremy Bakker, Steffani Kizziar, and Joanna Bradley served as indispensable editors.

And, of course, those family members who have shared my life most closely have offered me endless compassion—particularly Steffani Kizziar, Hannah Dreitcer, Monica Dreitcer, and Wendy Dreitcer.

The individuals whose stories I relate in this book have taught me more than they have known. Any names that appear apart from those noted above are pseudonyms to preserve the privacy or protection of those named. For similar reasons, some situations have been disguised.

Finally, I hope that I have accurately represented whatever I have received from the individuals who have graced my life. I am thankful for all they have given me. And if their gifts are misrepresented within these pages in any way, the fault is not theirs but entirely mine.

Longing for Compassion

Love your enemies. Do good to them . . . .
Be compassionate, just as God is compassionate.
–Luke 6:35, 36, AP

I was furious. My archenemy had been tormenting me for months—no, years. And now he was backing away from me, egging me on, daring me to punch him. I took the bait, advancing with a warrior stance, fists up, chin out, head high. We moved slowly around the arena, weaving through the crowds of stunned onlookers. My antagonist continued to backpedal, a mocking smile on his face, occasionally calling out an insult. And I continued my methodical pursuit, internally debating my strategy, seeking the most effective strike angle, aware that my height and reach exceeded his, reveling in my rage.

And in the midst of all this fury, this rush to vengeance, something else suddenly came to me, something I was trying to avoid, a voice in my head: *Love your enemies.*

What? *Love your enemies?* Where did that come from?

Actually, its source was clear: Sunday school, church, and my parents. After all, I was only ten years old. And I was a good Christian boy, a *very* good Christian boy. But in that moment, I wasn't acting like a good Christian boy at all. Instead, I was at war. Or at least I felt like I was at war. In reality, I was at recess. I was at recess in my tiny, rural Indiana elementary school. The "battlefield" was the school gymnasium. Decades before, this gym had been the home of weekly Hoosier high school basketball games, but now it was just a large, dilapidated room with scuffed, warping wooden floors and a few rows of grey bleachers along one wall. The "stunned onlookers" were just the other kids pausing for a moment from the frenzied running, yelling, and laughing that filled our twenty-minute break from classes. They wanted no part of whatever I was doing; they just wanted to avoid getting into trouble. And my "archenemy" was Donnie Sherman, poor little Donnie Sherman. Donnie was the middle child in a family of seven kids whose parents were barely keeping food on the table. He was small and weak and not much of a physical threat. Did any of that matter to me? No. Donnie had just said rude things about my father—again—and after endlessly taking his verbal abuse, I'd had enough. I lost it.

Well, that's not exactly true. I didn't *completely* lose it. In the end, I couldn't bring myself to hit Donnie Sherman. I just kept walking toward him, fists up and ready to strike, advancing and threatening, on and on—until a teacher intervened and sent us off to see the principal. So I never did punch Donnie Sherman. That pesky "love your enemies" voice wouldn't let me. I simply couldn't shake Jesus' commandment. Even my ten-year-old-boy fury couldn't overcome that teaching: *Love your enemies.*

For me, "love your enemies" was the highest standard of what it means to live the Christian life. It was what Christ did on the cross. As the gospel story goes, not only did Jesus heal the sick, feed the hungry, and free the prisoners, but he also forgave those who crucified him—he loved his enemies. And so should I, I was told.

Parental instructions and admonitions, as well as sermons and Sunday school curricula for all ages, very clearly tried to convince me to act in love. Adults showed me exemplary models of people who were loving. They took me on mission trips to give me opportunities to act in love. They gave me on-the-fly guidance in what love looks like: "Even if your little sister hits you, you are not to hit her back!" "Be kind, be generous." "Don't let the sun go down on your anger." "Do unto others as you would have others do unto you." "Go and do likewise." "No matter what Donnie Sherman does or says, don't punch him." "Do what Jesus would do: Love your enemy!" "No matter how unloving you might feel as you act lovingly, just do it."

And that was what I'd been doing with Donnie Sherman from the moment I had met him. I knew he was a mean boy bent on making my life miserable. Now, fifty years later, I imagine Donnie's nastiness toward me was his way of getting my attention because he wanted to be my friend. That nuance was lost on me at the time. He just seemed mean. But I had decided to love this enemy of mine no matter what he did because that is what I'd been taught. I knew it was true. Until I finally (nearly) lost it with Donnie at recess, I "loved my enemy" for years by gritting my teeth and bearing it. I was kind to him, never bad-mouthed him, and never told him what I really thought of him. Instead, I smiled and tried to ignore his meanness. I even defended him to my friends and parents when they spoke ill of him.

In the end, it didn't work. I didn't *feel* loving. No matter how much I tried to *act* in loving ways, to follow Jesus' invitation, I ultimately couldn't hold on to what I'd been taught I was supposed to do. I didn't know how to do it. I knew *what* to aim for but not *how* to get there. During that recess, confronted by Donnie Sherman's taunting, my anger and frustration overrode my belief-based resolve. My raised fists and threatening advance blew away my cover.

I'd like to say that after my cover was blown I learned my lesson with the Donnie Sherman incident. I wish I could tell you that the trip to the principal's office straightened me out and that for the past fifty years I've been a paragon of loving feelings and actions.

Alas, that didn't exactly happen. It's true that I've kept *trying* to love my enemies, all those other Donnie Shermans I've encountered. I've held onto Jesus' teaching my whole life. But again and again I have fallen short, for until recently I viewed Christian love as something I do despite myself, despite any unloving inclinations I may have. That is, no matter how I feel about someone, I am to *act* lovingly because that is my responsibility, the thing I know to be true, the thing I am commanded to do. In other words, true Christian love means ignoring the way I may feel and acting the way I know I should. It means willing myself to be loving no matter what. Faking it, just doing it, just acting lovingly can work well for a while.

Ultimately, however, there is a price to pay for this stance. I will hurt other people. My calm, caring demeanor toward the intended recipient of my loving actions may suddenly explode into rage; harbored resentments and frustrations cannot be contained. Just ask Donnie Sherman.

Other people are not the only ones who suffer from my inability to genuinely "love my enemies." I may also hurt myself. The constant efforts to manufacture acts of love because my faith demands it—even when I don't feel loving—may lead me to a sense of guilty inadequacy, or a sense of failure, or ultimately to burnout. Burnout sabotages all my efforts to live out the love to which I have committed my life.

A friend of mine describes this painful process in terms of trying to hold a buoy under water with my hands.[1] I keep the buoy submerged so that everything visible on the surface is smooth and calm. But eventually the buoy pops up, just as resentments boil over, rage flares, exhaustion or illness flattens me, and everyone sees the "shameful" reality that I am not who I appear to be. Yes, this painful process has been my experience for much of my life. Perhaps you have experienced something similar.

The Christian spiritual tradition invites us down a different path. Fortunately, over the past few years my colleagues and loved ones have helped me come to new understandings about this path, Jesus' invitation to love.

One new understanding I've come to is this: We don't have to conjure up love; love fills the core of our beings. The radical love at the heart of Christianity flows through every part of our lives. It nourishes our inner lives as we help nourish the world. It allows our outward acts of service to be authentic expressions of our inner lives. This is the spiritual path into which Jesus invites us, to lives in which love inhabits every part of our experience—our intentions, thoughts, feelings, and actions.

I have also come to understand that the heart of Jesus' invitation to love is an invitation to *compassion*—to live compassionately. We'll soon explore this notion at some length, but for now it's important to note that in the Christian scriptures and in Christian history, *love* is defined largely in terms of *compassion*. That's a relief to me. I confess I've never found it easy to define *love*. It's so very *big*. I can call it *agape* or say it's some complex mash-up of romantic, platonic, and unconditional stuff, but in the end, a precise definition of *love* eludes me. *Love* simply covers too much territory.

Compassion, though, gives me a handle on the massive umbrella that is love. According to Christian understandings, *compassion* refers to the concrete ways love (divine and human) is expressed. Compassion grounds love in the world we know. In human lives, compassion shows up as a combination of understanding, feeling, and acting that can be described, identified, named, precisely cultivated, and studied not only in daily life and communities of faith but also in theological studies and scientific laboratories. From this point on, I will speak of Christian love primarily in terms of compassion to help focus us more clearly on the heart of that difficult-to-define thing called *love*.[2]

The third new understanding that's come to me is this: The heart of the Christian path of love—radical compassion—can be *taught*. Loving compassion doesn't look like a version of my good-Christian-boy efforts with Donnie Sherman. I don't have to disregard my feelings, grit my teeth, and just do it. Instead, I can learn *how* to do it, how to become more completely compassionate. What an immense relief! Why? Because I long for my feelings to truly match the acts of compassion I believe I should perform. Wouldn't it be helpful, satisfying, inspiring, even motivating if my exterior acts of loving compassion reflected my interior experience? And wouldn't my behavior be more genuinely compassionate if it flowed from—rather than contradicted—my interior emotions?

You may have experienced such moments yourself, times in which your compassionate actions match your beliefs and deep feelings. Perhaps this unity happens when you see a small child crying in pain. You feel an immediate, spontaneous compassion, a desire to care for her, to ease her pain. And if possible, you will take some action to comfort her. (It's no surprise that entire fundraising campaigns are built on our compassionate reactions to images of suffering children.) You may have thought, *If only I could sustain this kind of compassion. If only I could learn how to more fully and genuinely live as the person I long to be.* But as I have suggested, it is possible to learn to be genuinely compassionate; compassion *can* be taught.

Unfortunately, religious and spiritual communities have not been able to draw much attention lately to their ability to grow compassion for the good of the world. Today, the spotlight on compassion shines mostly from a source that many do not always associate with compassion: scientists. A growing number of scientists are shaping their research in response to their personal desire to grow compassion for the good of the world. They have theorized that compassion may mitigate conflicts as well as offer mental and physical health benefits. As a result, scientific laboratories in several major universities around the world are developing programs of meditative practice to understand, cultivate, and sustain compassion. These programs have been careful to focus on the cultivation of compassion as something available to human beings in general rather than as something tied to religious or spiritual traditions. Researchers have found compelling evidence that compassion is an innate characteristic of human beings (and some other mammals as well) that has been essential to the survival of our species. Human beings have a "compassionate instinct."[3] Compassion is in our genes.

With this scientific data in hand, the creators of most compassion-cultivation programs describe their approach as secular or humanistic rather than religious—though they acknowledge that the compassion-cultivation practices they teach are derived from ancient Buddhist contemplative traditions.[4] The creators of these compassion-formation programs have intentionally secularized traditional Buddhist meditative practices by setting aside the language and concepts of Buddhism to highlight precisely what the meditators are doing technically during the practices. In this way, the researchers and teachers have made their compassion-training programs accessible to a wider audience than the programs might have reached had they been closely tied to a religious tradition. Further, by correlating results of brain scans, neurochemical analyses, behaviors, facial-response analyses, heart monitors, self-reporting, and other indicators, scientists have been able to begin identifying exactly what dimensions of spiritual practices correlate with the sustained formation of compassion. In other words, they are finding that compassion can be taught, and they are fine-tuning how to teach it.

These compassion-formation scientists have been doing extraordinarily valuable work; the world needs more compassion, emerging from all possible sources. Their work has prompted me to wonder about my own tradition, Christianity. Yes, ancient Buddhist traditions and secularized versions of those traditions have compassion-formation practices that can be taught, it seems, with identifiable success. But does Christianity? If so, what are they? Where would I find them? Could they really help us become more compassionate? Would ancient or traditional practices work for twenty-first-century Christians? Or are they so tied to specific times and places that present-day Christians (particularly those reading this book), seekers, and others would find them alien, incomprehensible, off-putting, or ineffective? And if the practices did come across as inaccessible, how could they be taught in such a way that they would be accessible and effective?

Before we begin to tackle such questions, let me tell you the bad news about traditional Christian compassion practices: There aren't any. None. As far as I know, there are no classical or traditional Christian practices that have been specifically identified or named as compassion-formation practices.

But here's the good news: even though there is nothing traditionally called a compassion practice in Christianity, compassion formation shows up everywhere. In fact, the purpose of virtually every Christian spiritual practice is, at least in part, the formation of compassion—because these practices are designed to help form people in the "image of God." According to Christian tradition, God's nature includes limitless, radical compassion, endless love. "God is love" (1 John 4:8); to live into the image of God is to become loving as God is loving, compassionate as God is compassionate. Even when Christian spiritual practices do not mention compassion at all, they carry an assumption that to engage them is to become more compassionate since that is an inescapable characteristic of being made in the loving image of God.

Compassion formation lies at the heart of virtually all Christian spiritual practices. What's more, some of these practices specifically identify compassion as their goal. In other words, certain practices are explicitly compassion-formation practices, even though they are not called "compassion practices." And, as we will see, these practices uniquely highlight aspects of compassion formation that other spiritual traditions do not. Unfortunately, people (including Christians) interested in compassion formation generally are not aware of what the Christian traditions offer them.

That is where this book comes in. I want to explore with you the ways certain Christian spiritual practices are "compassion practices," practices meant to help us feel, think, act, and *live* compassionately—in sustained, authentic ways.

You may be familiar with the compassion-forming practices we will explore since many people throughout the world have used them in one

form or another over the centuries. In fact, the oldest—the Jesus Prayer—
arose 1,500 years ago in North Africa and the Middle East. These practices offer a rich taste of how Christians over the ages have formed lives
of compassion. But their ancient perspectives may not match modern
sensibilities. I wonder, for instance, if my twenty-first-century, male,
North-American, white, Protestant experience of the world has much
of anything in common with the life experience of the Christian sages
throughout history who have shaped the practices we will explore. The
language that spiritual leaders of the past used to describe their practices—as well as their assumptions about such things as the structure
of the universe, relationships between men and women, religious traditions other than Christianity, and images of the Divine—can be con-
fusing, off-putting, and even offensive to present-day hearts and minds.
To explore these practices, we will need to be clear about the meanings
of key terms I will be using, including *compassion* itself. Over the ages
this term and others related to it have taken on many nuances of meaning because of translations and the varying influences of cultures. It will
be important to not only understand these terms generally but also to
understand what they mean in relation to the particular practices we will
explore and in connection to our own unique life experiences.

Finally, before turning to the practices that are the focus of this book,
we will need to understand a bit about the dynamics of how spiritual practices work. That is, certain patterns are built into the fabric of spiritual
practices and appear repeatedly across traditions. We can, for instance,
identify how someone engaged in a practice is expected (according to
the practice tradition's teaching) to respond to feelings, thoughts, mental pictures, physical sensations, and urges (all the "interior stuff") that
emerge during the practice. When considering engaging in any practice,
I can ask myself, *What is to be my stance toward the thoughts, feelings,
images, and sensations that run through my awareness while I am in the
practice? What am I to do with them when they appear? How am I to
respond to them (or not)?* Understanding answers to such questions helps
us gain as much as we can from what the practices offer.

Before concluding this introduction, I want to emphasize that we
will not explore compassion-formation practices simply for the sake of
understanding them for what they are (though that is not a bad thing).

Rather, we will mine them for what they offer for the shaping of our own lives and glean from them timeless lessons about how compassion can be formed in our current world. As I have suggested, the ancient practices present us with language and worldviews that may not make sense to the sensibilities of contemporary North Americans. A practice developed for monks in medieval Italy may make little sense for, say, an elementary-school teacher in twenty-first-century Omaha or a software developer in Silicon Valley. Ultimately, I will translate these ancient contemplative processes into practices that are more accessible to us, practices that can more easily form compassion in our own lives here and now.

My concern for practical relevancy will turn us again and again to a compassion-formation process that has arisen within the past decade. This process, called the Compassion Practice, draws from traditional Christian contemplative practices, contemporary psychological under-standings, and current scientific research. Spiritual practices and exer-cises connected to the Compassion Practice will be sprinkled throughout this book—including within the "Review and Practice" sections at the end of each chapter. These exercises and practices will include contem-porary expressions of ancient practices that have formed compassion in the lives of Christians over the ages. They will also gradually introduce the movements of the Compassion Practice itself, culminating in a pre-sentation of the entire process. I invite you to enter into these exercises as you feel drawn.

The Compassion Practice can revolutionize how we understand com-passion. But more importantly, it leads us to uncover and express the innate compassion within us, turning our desire for compassion into a life centered in compassion, a compassion that is genuine and abiding. In other words, the Compassion Practice can teach us how to love our neighbors, ourselves, and, yes, even our enemies.

Review and Practice

Genuine compassion does not consist of "just doing it," faking it, or forcing yourself to act the way you have been told you are supposed to act. It does not mean loving your enemy despite what you feel. Instead, true compassion means your actions and interior experiences mirror one another and flow from one another. Spiritual traditions have created practices to help fill your life ever more completely with this compassion.

The process of filling our lives with compassion begins with recognizing our deep longing for this profound human experience. The longing for compassion appears in human beings whether they are part of a spiritual tradition or not. According to the Christian spiritual path, this longing is not our *own* desire—it is Divine Mystery, God, the eternal Source of Compassion longing through our entire being. We begin to expand compassion in our lives by engaging this Divine longing within us. We may then return repeatedly to taste this longing, allowing it to draw us ever more deeply into the Compassion at the heart of our being.

A Compassion Practice: Longing for Compassion

- At the beginning of the day, pose these questions to yourself: *What does longing for compassion look like in my life? How does my longing for compassion feel?*
- Draw your attention toward this longing as you go through your day and acknowledge God's presence there.
- Throughout the day, where do you notice longing for compassion? What do you notice about it? When does it show up most easily? Most frequently? What sparks it? What events, people, moments, situations, contexts awaken it? What sustains this longing? What inhibits it?
- At the end of the day, review. Notice where longing for compassion has appeared. You may ask yourself: *Where, how, when did I least experience longing in this day? Where, how, when did I most experience longing in this day?*
- Write a statement, reflection, or prayer that expresses what has arisen for you in this time.

CHAPTER 1

Becoming Compassion

I am blessed with two wise daughters, Hannah and Monica. These two accomplished women have taught me a great deal over their twenty-plus years; they've been teaching me since the moment they were born. Monica, for instance, taught me a spiritual truth that has shaped my life forever, and she did it only a few months after she drew her first breath.

At the time, two-year old Hannah, tiny Monica, their mother, and I lived in a two-room, walk-up apartment. Each room served double or triple duty. The kitchen sink was too small for a plate. The only space for a refrigerator was outside the back door. These were student digs; I was studying full-time in a PhD program. I was also directing a seminary spirituality program part-time, serving as a part-time co-pastor with my wife, and sharing childcare duties. I was always tired, and my spiritual life was taking a hit.

Not many years before, I had spent twelve months living at a monastery. During the thrice-daily common prayer times in the darkened church, I had experienced a sense of being held in quiet warmth. Retreat weeks helped me find rejuvenating rest in Divine Mystery. The rhythms of that contemplative community tied my spirituality to the sacred trinity of silence, solitude, and sleep.

My new trinity of jobs, family, and studies left no time or energy for the contemplative practices to which I had become accustomed. But one late night as I was rocking newborn Monica and longing for the monastery's quiet, warm solitude, an awareness began to grow. I began to pay attention to my surroundings.

What I noticed was this: I was sitting in a darkened, warm place, surrounded by silence; I was sharing a time of communal solitude with the tiny person in my arms; I was feeling a deep, rejuvenating rest, a kind of waking sleep. Here was a new version of silence, solitude, and sleep—one fitting my changed situation. And I noticed something more: I had a sense of being held and rocked in loving compassion. Not only that, but I also felt that same sense of compassionate love for Monica. I was holding her in my arms of loving compassion.

This experience stays with me as a profound image of the nature of compassion. Perhaps you too have had a similar experience, a threefold circle of compassion: compassion *received* from the endless Source of Compassion called God; compassionate *feelings* for another being; and compassionate *actions* that lead to another's flourishing. I received compassion in my sense of being held and rocked. I felt compassion in my deep sense of love for Monica. I acted compassionately when I held and rocked Monica.

Experiences like these teach us what compassion is. I know compassion most fully not because someone has defined the word for me in a graduate-school course or because I looked it up on Wikipedia. I know compassion because I have felt it. So have you in the touch of a calming hand, the sound of a soothing voice, the warm soup made to ward off the cold, the words spoken on behalf of someone falsely accused . . . every time we notice compassion touching us, it expands, seeping into other situations and encounters, past, present, and future. In rocking Monica, I recalled similar times with her sister Hannah years before. That memory, in turn, carried compassion to moments yet to come.

Yes, as we move through daily life, we do not need to nail down a definition for *compassion*. We know compassion when we feel it. As I've noted, scientists are finding that we have an innate inclination toward compassion, a compassionate instinct. Compassion is in our bones.

Even though it's true that we know compassion, we struggle to define it clearly. If we desire to grow compassion in our lives, we must know what we're aiming for. If I want compassion in my life, I need to be clear about the details of both the path and its destination. Therefore, I want to define more clearly what we already know in our bones.

The Meaning of Compassion

What does *compassion* mean? No one has tried to answer that question more clearly than the scientists studying compassion formation. Many of these researchers have adopted this definition: *Compassion* is "the feeling that arises when you are confronted with another's suffering and feel motivated to relieve that suffering." Here compassion consists of *feelings*. One feeling that arises when we notice someone suffering is *empathy*. *Empathy* is "the ability to take the perspective of and feel the emotions of another person." Another feeling comes in the form of desire, a sense of being motivated to help.[1]

Notice that this definition of compassion does not include actions to help people. Helpful actions may come from compassion, but they aren't included within the definition of compassion itself. Instead, scientists tend to define these helpful actions as *altruism*. Sometimes altruistic actions flow from compassion. Sometimes they happen apart from compassion. Due to this distinction, scientists study the actions of altruism in addition to studying the feelings of compassion. Some Buddhist, psychological, and popular notions about the relationship between compassion and altruism closely match these scientific understandings.[2]

At the outset, I want to be clear that I am not leading with scientific, popular, or Buddhist definitions of compassion to suggest that these are any better or worse than other understandings of the term. However, I want to make sure that when we notice references to compassion we are careful to note what understanding lies behind them. Scientific definitions offer one example of the meaning of compassion. One definition of a term is not necessarily better than another. As we continue to explore compassion in this book, it is important to keep in mind that the definition of compassion in Christian traditions includes a range of things that other traditions may name with other terms. Remembering this fact can help us make grace-filled connections across traditions. What's more, if we want to learn how certain Christian spiritual practices teach us to be compassionate, we need to know as fully as possible what we are aiming for and what being compassionate looks like.

That brings us to the Christian understanding of compassion. Christians across the ages have viewed compassion as a central characteristic of the nature of God, the life of Jesus of Nazareth, and the life of the faithful Christian—whether they use the word *compassion* or not. But what is compassion in the Christian tradition? As with all matters of Christian tradition, we begin with scripture.

The Characteristics of Compassion in the Bible

In the Bible, genuine compassion contains three characteristics that inseparably intertwine: understanding, feeling, and acting.

In Christian scriptures, the *understanding* of compassion comes from teachings of the Hebrew scriptures and of Jesus. The people hear and see God's compassion, human compassion, and the importance of following the path of compassion.

The *feeling* of compassion found in the Bible is a spontaneous, empathetic response of deep and abiding care. The roots of the words most commonly translated into English as *compassion* convey an instinctive, emotion-filled, physical churning of the gut or a maternal movement of the womb.[3] This body-based emotion is a feeling of sharing in the experience of another person. That sense of connection comes across when we divide the word into its Latin segments and translate those segments back into English: *passion*=feeling; *com*=with.

Understandings and feelings, however, don't stand alone in biblical texts about compassion. Whenever words for compassion appear in the Bible, *actions* to ease suffering are sure to follow. As the best translations of the biblical texts put it, we are *moved* to compassion. Compassion is dynamic—both in the movements of feelings within us and in the movements of our actions in the world. We don't *have* compassion; we *become* compassionate.

Three characteristics of compassion come to fruition in Jesus' parable of the Good Samaritan (Luke 10:25-37): loving God, loving yourself, and loving others. Before Jesus tells the parable, a lawyer tests him by asking him what he must "do to inherit eternal life" (Luke 10:25). The question challenges Jesus to state the meaning and purpose of Jewish law and all of life. But Jesus turns the challenge back on the man, essentially asking him how he would answer his own question. The man responds with what Jesus says is the right *understanding*: Love God with your entire being, and love your neighbor as yourself (a conflation of Deut. 6:5 and Lev. 19:18).

After the lawyer asks Jesus, "Who is my neighbor?" (Luke 10:29), Jesus tells a story about a man who was robbed, beaten, and left by the road "half dead" (Luke 10:30). The injured man's religious leaders, his models and teachers in the spiritual life, those he honors, those who should care for him, pass by without helping him.

Then along comes a Samaritan, a citizen of an enemy nation, seemingly the last person who might help this dying traveler. The Samaritan, says Jesus in the passage, is moved to compassion; he becomes compassion. He experiences an emotional churning of the gut, deeply *feeling* the wounded man's pain. And then the Samaritan, *understanding* what he is called to do in this situation, *acts* to ease the pain, binding his enemy's wounds and caring for him until he is healed. This core teaching of Jesus shows us that to become fully compassionate is to turn appropriate understanding and care-filled feeling into purposeful, caring actions.

Biblical Compassion: A Circle of Relationships

Before leaving the Good Samaritan story, I want to note one other thing the passage shows us: In the Bible, compassion is a circle of relationships. The core elements of compassion—understanding, feeling, and actions— only have life and meaning within that circle of the eternal Source of Compassion, others, and self. The relationship with the Divine Source of Compassion shows up in Jesus' invitation to "love God." The compassionate relationship with others appears in Jesus' call to ". . . love your neighbor." And Jesus' invitation to "love yourself" (Luke 10:27) reveals the relationship of self-compassion.

The first relationship in this circle comes as we connect with God's Presence, the sacred Source of Compassion. The various Christian traditions name this compassionate Presence in a multitude of ways: Christ, Holy Spirit, Father, Mother, Light, Word, God beyond God, Ground of Being, Being Itself. To highlight the centrality of compassion in Christian theological understandings, I favor referring to God with names such as Eternal Compassion, Divine Compassion, Presence of Compassion—or simply Compassion (note the capital C). But no matter how we name the Eternal Sour⸻assion, to love God is to love resting in God's compassionate ⸻ love God is to love God's compassion flowing in, through, ⸻ entire world in a way that grounds and enlivens all that is.

I experienced this compassionate Presence when I was rocking Monica. I loved the sense of being held, myself, in loving arms, and I loved how that Divine Love flowed to Monica through me and back to Love. The Compassion that is Divine Presence offers us comfort, healing, and restoration wherever we need it. Yes, Divine Compassion flows to the Donnie Shermans in our lives, those people we think of as working against the Presence of Love. It even flows to the movements within ourselves that we experience as shameful, undeserving, or destructive. This boundless Source of Compassion is the heart of the good news.

Another relationship in the circle of compassion comes in our connection with others, the neighbor, the people, and the entire world beyond ourselves. Our own experiences of Divine Compassion free us to be compassionate. Through our compassionate love for others, God's compassionate love expands and deepens in ways we can never fully plan for or envision.

When I was holding Monica, there was no separation between the compassion I felt for her and the compassion I felt from God. Christianity has always insisted that there can be no love of God in the absence of loving others and vice versa. Further, *neighbor* is not merely those near and dear to us or those who care for us as we care for them. The opposite is true. *Neighbor* includes the "distant other," even those experienced as enemy. The gospel stories portray Jesus defining love of neighbor in terms of the relationship of active compassion between a "good" Samaritan and a Jew, members of groups set on maintaining mutual loathing.

The remaining relationship in the circle is compassion for self. If you share my experience of the Christian message, the first two relationships named in the circle of compassion may be familiar. Again and again I have heard that the Christian life, the life of compassion, involves the love of God and the love of neighbor. Sermons, Sunday-school lessons, and parents have conveyed that teaching to me above all others. But here's an odd thing: Seldom, if ever, have I heard anyone tell me I should compassionately love *myself*. In fact, the loudest message has been, "Turn to others and ignore yourself." Anything else is merely selfish.

Yet Jesus' love commandment invites precisely the opposite approach. It says to "love your neighbor *in the same way you love yourself and vice versa.*" The construction of the original Greek sentence makes *yourself* and *neighbor* interchangeable and inseparable. Self-compassion and compassion for others form one package.

This circle is what I experienced as I rocked Monica those many years ago. As I was tender toward her and as I sensed being held by a Source of Compassion, a gentle compassion toward myself began to grow. I could recognize my exhaustion and its sources. I began to see how I could use this nighttime "rocking-chair retreat" to restore my soul. And from that restored place I could more fully care for Monica.

Compassion for ourselves is vital for the Christian spiritual path. Fortunately, in the past few years, teachers, practitioners, and scholars have developed programs to teach and research self-compassion. These programs insist that compassion for others cannot fully blossom if we do not have compassion for ourselves—and research seems to support this claim. The practices in these programs echo the truths of the Good Samaritan story, even as they also draw from Buddhism and psychotherapy.[4]

Fortunately, the Christian tradition also includes forms of contemplative practice that focus on the development of self-compassion. In coming chapters, we will explore how the formation of self-compassion connects with the compassion of God and compassion for others. Until then, it is enough to keep in mind that self-compassion is an indispensable part of the circle of compassionate relationships described by the Good Samaritan passage. These circles have as vital a role to play in the twenty-first century as they did in the first.

Compassion Today

Some years ago, I was in a violence-torn country shortly after a pre-election, government-instigated campaign of terror. The president of the nation, as part of his reelection strategy, had commanded the killing and torturing of people who resisted voting for the ruling party. To control the election, government forces used money, alcohol, and torture to force young men—many of them teenagers—to go into their own villages and to kill, rape, and maim the people they had grown up with.

In the wake of the atrocities of that campaign, I had been invited to participate in the first public event for healing and reconciliation in that country. Friends of mine—staff members of a spiritually based social-services center in the country—had organized the conference around the theme of compassion, healing, and reconciliation in situations of conflict.

Over ninety people showed up for the conference, most having traveled with great difficulty over long distances. The event organizers welcomed religious leaders, tribal chiefs, and victims of torture, many whose fingers had been cut off or who carried scars from being beaten because they hadn't voted for the president of the country.

All the conference participants had watched young men of their villages commit horrible atrocities against neighbors, family, friends, and loved ones. Now that the elections were over and the government had retained its power, these young men had few options but to return to their homes. They lived as pariahs in the villages that had raised them. Against great odds the men and women at this event came together in the hope that they could find genuine compassion for the young men in their villages and for all other perpetrators of violence. They longed for the healing and reconciliation such compassion might bring, even as they were wracked by rage and grief.

As I pondered the horrors and hope represented within this gathering, I began to wonder: *How could the victims of such violence live next to its perpetrators? How could the tortured tolerate their torturers?* Yes, the tribal chiefs and Christian pastors at our conference belonged to traditions that embraced compassion toward even the most heinous of enemies, but was that truly possible? What could compassion mean for these spiritual leaders now that they were expected to welcome their enemies into their neighborhoods, their tribal gatherings, and their church services?

The conference center itself mirrored the struggles of those who gathered there. A Roman Catholic retreat center and convent, it looked solid and attractive. But there was no electricity; we had to end our daily gatherings before dark. And there was no fuel for cooking; the nuns fixed our meals over fires built from wood gathered from surrounding fields.

These challenges slowed no one down. During the four days of the conference, I watched in awe as the participants entered compassion practices for individuals, for relationships, and for the healing of broken communities. Along the way, they not only refined the practices (which inform exercises within the Compassion Practice found in this book), but also they honed my understanding of what compassion means in real lives in today's world. They showed how compassion contains two elements that many of us may overlook: *wisdom* and *restoration*.

Compassion is *wise*. True compassion is grounded in spontaneous feeling, informed by understanding, and expressed in action, as our look at biblical understandings of compassion showed. But these core elements must be infused with wisdom: thoughtful analysis, careful deliberation, and spiritual discernment informed by intuition, data, and prayerful attention to divine invitation.[5]

Without wisdom, reactions to compassionate feelings can lead to actions that may not actually be compassionate—that is, they may not be in the best interests of the persons they are meant to help. Without wisdom, understanding can merely skim the surface and focus on problem-solving activities rather truly meeting persons' needs. Unwise action, no matter how caring the intention, may be misguided, inappropriate, or even harmful.

Have you ever acted out of a spontaneous desire to help others, only to learn later that they didn't want that kind of help? Perhaps all they wanted was your understanding presence or to be alone or to make their own mistakes to learn something new in life. I, for one, offer this kind of help all too often, as my family would be quick to tell you. Fortunately, they don't hesitate to remind me to be a bit wiser.

The compassion conference facilitated the formation of wisdom-filled compassion. Wisdom grew as the pastors, Christian lay leaders, and tribal chiefs moved through a process of deep reflection on their lives and contexts. The process consisted of information-based, heartfelt storytelling combined with compassionate listening. And it led to discerning analysis of all that is evoked within us as we confront injustice, pain, and trauma.

As the conference unfolded, the participants told one another their stories, and they listened, truly listened. The stories were difficult to tell and to hear.

Paul, a young pastor with a wife and children, stood and boldly described a horrific night during the elections. The government had conscripted a group of young men from his village into playing the role of thugs. The group demanded that Paul support the ruling party. When he refused, they beat him with sticks wrapped with barbed wire and dragged him to a slaughterhouse. There, another group beat him with a stone and left him for dead. Late that night some women found him lying unconscious and bleeding. They lifted him into a wheelbarrow and carried him to a hospital. His tormentors came to the hospital and demanded he be released to them. The nurses saved Paul's life by saying he wasn't there. When Paul finally returned home after weeks in the hospital, he discovered that the thugs had destroyed his family's crops, burned their house to the ground, and taken all their food. Paul's great blessing was that his wife and children had escaped unharmed.

An older woman told another story about refusing to agree to vote for the ruling party. Government thugs—again, young men from her own village—cut off her finger to keep her from voting. Without that finger's print, she could not prove her identity at the polls.

I listened, stunned, to these and other stories that filled the conference space—descriptions of torture, abuse, and other acts of targeted violence—as people stood one at a time to speak their truths. The speakers had never had the chance to share these experiences before, to be heard and honored. The group responded to the stories in silence or with prayer or singing. This stance of compassionate listening allowed information-filled truth-telling to unfold, a data-gathering dimension of wisdom. This was a clarifying, cleansing, cathartic time, but the participants knew they needed more wisdom work.

That work continued as the participants spent time alone in meditation and personal reflection. I watched them sitting, standing, walking, and kneeling as they scattered around the grounds of the conference facility, silently identifying their deepest thoughts and feelings, gathering information about themselves, and exploring their heartfelt responses to the stories they had heard.

They re-gathered to share what they had found within themselves. A middle-aged man stood, shaking, and said, "I am filled with rage." A young woman called out, "I want revenge!" Another woman raised her voice to say only, "Tears." Other voices added to the chorus: "Hatred." . . . "Sadness." . . . "I can't hear any more of this." . . . "I want justice!"

Eventually, after the voices died down, one of the conference organizers invited us to notice the deep hopes and longings attached to the pains that everyone had named. Again, voices arose one at a time. "I want to feel safe again," said a young man. "I hope our village can be united again," said a distinguished tribal chief. "I want to be able to have compassion for the people who beat me," said another.

Throughout this time of speaking thoughts and feelings, conference leaders reminded us how vital it is to name these painful parts of ourselves and to pay empathy-filled attention to our own responses and to those of others by being present and listening without judgment.

The entire gathering embraced this thoughtful, discernment-filled exploration of inner experiences and then added a final layer of wisdom: practical information about their situation gathered through intuition, social analysis, and prayerful attention to Divine invitation. Soon, groups of five or six people began forming in and around the meeting area. Each cluster contained a mix of tribal leaders and Christian leaders from the same geographic area, men and women, young and old, wearing neckties and khakis, colorful dresses and scarves, or tribal robes and caps.

Subdued murmurs alternated with laughs and animated conversations as each group's members reviewed what they had already discovered about themselves and their situations. They sought to understand the specific, data-filled details of one another's family, community, and village. They identified their personal challenges and those of their communities. They bowed heads together, meditated, and prayed.

Slowly and steadily, through their social analysis, reflection, non-judgmental listening, and prayer, the members of the gathering came back to the reason they had come to the conference in the first place: to discover how to be compassionate to those they experienced as enemies. One by one they recounted their deepest intentions, motivations, and dreams for themselves, their communities, and those who had harmed them.

One pastor's words captured the group's focus. He reviewed how the government had coerced, forced, or lured the young men of his village into raping, maiming, and killing people in the community. Now that the government-driven terror campaign had ended, those young men had nowhere to go but home—back to the victims of their violence. "How am I to forgive them?" the pastor asked tearfully. "How are we to love them as Jesus does? How are we to be compassionate?"

Hushed conversations unfolded as this gathering of committed spiritual and community leaders shared stories like the pastor's. One woman recalled Jesus' invitation to compassion. Another remembered the young men of her own community as they had been when they were small children. She recalled how those boys had grown into hopelessness and despair and finally surrendered to offers of money, alcohol, and shelter—only to discover it was all a trap.

Together and in solitude the members of the conference attended to the pain of those who had caused them pain. In this way, they began to re-experience the compassion deep within themselves, compassion that had been hidden beneath the fears and defenses needed to keep themselves and their loved ones safe. The wisdom required for genuine compassion had now matured: Here was clear, real-world information combined with empathy-filled understanding of themselves and others.

Up to this point my friends at the conference had expanded their wisdom through social analysis, and probing, and personal reflection. This expanded wisdom then led us to understand that genuine compassion is not only wise but *restorative*. Compassion is not the same as "niceness." Nor is it weak. Compassion is wisely-shaped, informed, "feeling-with" behavior that will take the form of tough love or gentleness depending on the situation. Genuine compassion requires courage, accountability, clarity, and truth. Compassion does not try to answer some version of "What will help everyone feel good?" Nor does it demonize or denigrate those who cause harm, no matter how horrible their actions may have been. Compassion does not seek retribution. Rather, it aims for what will help bring true healing, vitality, and freedom to all involved, victims and perpetrators alike.

Everyone at the conference was now committed to this transformative vision of engaged compassion. In the final day of the gathering, the participants developed strategies for compassion-based, restorative justice within every geographical area they represented.[6]

Again, conference participants divided into small groups based on where they lived. Tribal leaders and Christian leaders from the same villages began to brainstorm programs and projects to meet the unique needs of their communities. Poster board covered the walls. The sounds of charged conversations and the scent of colored markers filled the room as the groups hashed out ideas and drew up lists. Groups spent hours strategizing and organizing for the future of compassion in their communities. Then each group reported its plan to the entire gathering. Every plan addressed the needs of both victims and perpetrators.

What did the plans for strong, restorative compassion require of those who had been harmed? Compassion required a genuine openness of heart and a true desire for brokenness to be repaired in victims and perpetrators. This took several forms, depending on the community. For one, it included a regular Bible study that explored the nature of God's compassion in scripture. For another, it involved establishing a counseling program to meet the spiritual, emotional, and physical needs of those who were grieving and for those who were traumatized in other ways. Whatever form the strategies for restoration took, each one included extended time for healing.

What about the perpetrators of violence? What did the plans for restorative compassion require of them? Everyone recognized that some of the young men who had returned to their home villages might need to spend time in prison to ensure that they were cared for and others were safe. At the very least, they would need focused programs for psychological, emotional, and spiritual rehabilitation. In all cases, restorative compassion required that these young men ask for forgiveness, admit the pain they had caused, and offer restitution as best they could and in ways acceptable to their victims. Only after all these requirements were met could the young men seek true forgiveness and the victims offer it. Only then could true healing and reconciliation begin to grow among everyone involved.

Everyone at the conference agreed that this was the first time the nation's tribal chiefs and Christian leaders had worked together for the good of their wider communities. Years after the conference, the plans these wise, compassionate folks put in place continued to bear fruit. Deep deliberation, analysis, and careful discernment turned understandings and feelings into effective actions.

The situation I encountered in that troubled country reminds us that in the Christian spiritual tradition, compassion is not a spontaneous reaction triggered by anguish over someone else's pain. Nor is it information-based understanding. Instead, true compassion transforms feelings and understandings into carefully discerned, practical, effective ways to change individual lives—and the world—for good.

For many people this path of wise, restorative compassion is a matter of life and death, just as it was for the wounded man in Jesus' parable of the Good Samaritan. The Samaritan assessed the situation, understood the need, formed a plan, and followed it through. He tended the man's wounds, found him a place to stay, and attended to him until he healed. My friends at the conference acted similarly in their communities through their discernment-filled planning and in the years after the conference.

You and I have opportunities for this kind of compassion every day of our lives, in ways great and small: with the coworker weeping because her marriage is in tatters, with the snarky teenager who has replaced the sparkly toddler who used to live here, with the homeless shelter down the street, with the longing you may have for a new and life-giving vocation. Fortunately, the great spiritual traditions show us a grace-filled truth, tested across the centuries: We can grow compassionate lives through practices meant for just that purpose.

Spiritual Capacities for Compassion

I've already described some of what I learned from my friends in the strife-torn country I visited, but there's more to that story. While this was the first time tribal chiefs, Christian leaders, and victims of government violence had publicly gathered in that nation, they were not the only participants invited. The organizers had asked the government to send official representatives. This invitation was another first, and it was a bold and potentially dangerous move. Normally, such a gathering was secret, but not this one. The conference leaders wanted all sides of the conflict—perpetrators and victims—to come together. Organizers planned for open proceedings. Transcripts of the conversations were sent to the government, and government officials were welcomed as part of the group.

Unfortunately, the conference organizers had received no RSVPs from the government. As the gathering began, we all assumed no representatives from the country's official hierarchy would be there. We soon discovered we were wrong. It turned out that the dozens of participants included two government representatives; however, they were hard to spot. Why? Because they came undercover, disguised as chaplains, evidently unable to trust that we would truly welcome them. They were members of the government's secret security force. They were spies. Everyone at the conference gradually realized who they were as understanding spread through whispered conversations.

During one compassion practice, each participant paired with a conversation partner. One of the spies was left alone; no one wanted to risk being with him. One of the conference leaders pointed to the man and said to me, "That's your partner, Andy. Go be with him." I shot a look that said, "Really? You know I hate that kind of sharing, especially with spies." But there was no way out. I was there to learn compassion, after all. And anyway, the assignment was simple enough to understand, though it wasn't easy to execute. The facilitators instructed us: Tell each other a story of a time when you experienced much pain. Without saying a word, listen to the other person tell a story of great pain. Feel compassion grow in you. Act with compassion. Be compassion.

I followed the directions. I shared the most painful event in my life, my late wife's unsuccessful fight against brain cancer when our daughters were in their early teens. I described months filled with surgeries and chemotherapy, physical agony, emotional turmoil, and my daughters and me watching their mother's last breaths as she lay in a bed where our dining-room table had normally stood. I did not gild the trauma. My spy buddy was completely silent. *Oh yeah*, I thought, *he looks like he's listening. But he's just a good actor. He's good at following orders.*

Then it was the spy's turn to talk. What he said stunned me. With tears in his eyes, he started describing vast reservoirs of pain, shame, and frustration. He spoke of fears about his marriage. He told of being unable to find a way to leave the work he did as part of the government's system of violence. He longed to be able to complete university courses that would open a new career for him. With a bit more money, he might find a way. But things seemed so hopeless. How could he begin a new life with no base to build from? It felt as if all he had in life was a quiet agony and a fear of the future. Because of his work, he could trust almost no one. And yet he poured out his story to me, a stranger from another land. He had so much to say that the exercise ended before he could finish. This prompted him to ask me to lunch—alone.

I accepted, and suddenly people were afraid for me. They warned me to stay away from him and asked me not to go. But I had been given my instructions: Be compassion.

Despite the warnings, my spy buddy and I went off to eat by ourselves. The first thing he did was blow his cover: He showed me his secret security-force I.D., his official spy documentation. Then he continued to share. He described how, in the face of devastating unemployment, he needed this job. He needed help providing care for his baby. He wanted to know how he could keep his family together, safe and secure. He hated what he had been trained to do. He wanted out. But if he tried to leave, he and his family might be tortured or killed.

In our conversation, he explored where he might find support. Eventually, he identified an older man of faithful integrity who might counsel and mentor him. As I continued to listen, this reluctant spy's imagination began to ignite. He began to describe other possibilities for his life; he described his dreams of going to school, the university courses he might take, a vocation that would help his family, the world, and him flourish. Then the lunch period ended. I had to return to my leadership responsibilities. However, my friend was not finished. He asked me to meet with him at the evening meal, but by that afternoon he was gone.

In my time with my new friend, I had seen great fear, but I also had seen great hope. I do not know what happened to him, but I do know at least one thing: This man, my new friend, was trained to inflict fear and pain. But engaging in a compassion-forming exercise—a compassion practice—within a compassionate community opened him to the truth at the core of his being. It allowed him to be vulnerable, to be present, to feel and express love. It did a similar thing for me. Together, through this practice, we experienced ourselves and each other in a new way—a way of compassion.

Christian spiritual traditions trust that compassion practices change people in the way my conference spy friend and I were changed. But how? What is it about the nature of certain spiritual practices that move people to compassion?

To answer this question, we need to explore what exactly we are doing when we engage in a practice. That means we'll look at some spiritual practices, but before we get to those, we need to see something of what goes on inside us when we engage in spiritual practices. That is, we'll look at certain muscles of our inner world—certain spiritual capacities—that get an active workout through spiritual practices.

Think of spiritual capacities as muscles of the interior life that do the work of the practice and grow stronger in the process. A weight-training regimen of lifting twenty pounds will shape your body over time as it bulks up the muscles that do the lifting. Our spiritual muscles, the spiritual capacities, get stronger as we use them. Our spiritual lives take on new shapes the stronger the capacities get.

In the forming of compassion, the spiritual capacities come in two varieties: Foundational Capacities and Compassion Capacities.

- The Foundational Capacities establish a base, a foundation on which to build compassion. They are *intention, awareness,* and *attention.*
- The Compassion Capacities build compassion on the foundation laid by the Foundational Capacities. The Compassion Capacities are *feelings, intimacy,* and *imagination.*

We'll first look at the Foundational Capacities before turning to the Compassion Capacities.

The Foundational Capacities: Intention, Awareness, and Attention

The best way to explore the Foundational Capacities is to look at a practice, and the practice we'll examine is driving a car. Granted, driving is not necessarily a *spiritual* practice (though it could be), but it takes many of the same human capacities to learn to drive a car as it does to enter any spiritual practice.

This fact was driven home to me when my daughter Monica asked me to teach her how to drive a stick shift. Her aunt had loaned her a beater car (a twenty-five-year-old Volvo station wagon) so that Monica would have a way to get to work each day. Fortunately, Monica had been driving for nine years; unfortunately, she'd always driven an automatic. I, on the other hand, learned to drive at the wheel of an ancient, four-on-the-floor pickup on the farm when I was twelve years old. That made me the manual-transmission expert. Thus, I became a driving instructor for my twenty-five-year-old daughter.

I trust anyone can see the complexities of this arrangement with no prompting from me. But setting aside the challenges inherent in this particular situation, what can the practice of driving a car teach us about Foundational Capacities?

Let's start with *intention*. Monica's intention was clear: She needed to get to work; the Volvo was the only car available; she wanted lessons. Her intention to drive that car set up a chain of events in her interior life: her desire to gain the autonomy that would be achieved through driving lessons, regardless of who the instructor might be; her understandings and expectations about what was involved with taking lessons from her father, the Expert Driver; her willingness to take them from said father, the Expert Driver, anyway; her commitment to identifying a place to practice, get in the car, and drive with her father, the Expert Driver, in the passenger seat.

Similarly, I need intention to engage in a spiritual practice. In that case, the chain of events that follows my intention may be as short as spontaneously deciding I want to meditate, settling on the type of meditation and my expectations around it, and then choosing a spot on my sofa to do it. Or it may turn into finding a worship space for a thousand people, setting up the venue, finding musicians, advertising, planning the experience, and helping the participants understand the assumptions and expectations of the event.

What was the role of intention as it relates to my spy friend at the healing and reconciliation conference? Intention was there in the purpose of the compassion practice we shared: to give and receive caring empathy. As with driving a car, spiritual practices need intention—the process of consciously turning toward whatever the practice involves and being willing to let that process unfold.

Awareness is a second capacity we need when learning to drive a car and when engaging spiritual practices. As Monica found in her process of learning to drive a stick shift, the capacity of awareness usually starts out small and grows. Awareness refers to the ability to notice whatever is happening in any moment. Monica already knew she had to be aware of many things at once: the approaching stop sign, the truck visible in her right-side mirror, the location of the brake pedal, and the list goes on. She had to add the clutch and shift lever to that list. Getting fixated on one passing thing for very long—say, the four-foot-long iguana perched on the driver-side windowsill of the car in the next lane—would have derailed her original intention (learning to drive a stick shift), perhaps resulting in a dangerous outcome.

Similarly, many spiritual practices invite us to notice what is happening in each moment. "What is happening" includes movements in the external world such as cars honking, someone running across the street, or the smell of diesel exhaust. It also includes movements within us: thoughts, feelings, impulses, mental pictures, mental conversations— *What is the speed limit? . . . I hate these curves. . . . Brake now! . . . The clutch, the clutch! . . . I remember a stop sign at the bottom of this hill. . . . I've been driving for nine years . . . so I'm a good driver, aren't I? Good enough? Maybe not? . . . Clutch! Big iguana?! Brake! Down-shift!* In open awareness, we notice each thing that comes, internally and externally, but get fixated on none of them.

What does open awareness toward the internal world look like? At the compassion conference I attended, my spy friend and I were practicing open awareness as we told our stories to each other. During the telling, we did not rest on one memory at the expense of others. Each memory passed to the next as we shared in the stream of what was being said. One memory was voiced, heard, and then another took its place. In such a practice, awareness treats the flow of internal movements— including life memories recalled and spoken and heard—as if they are sites moving past us as we drive a car: noticing, releasing, repeating.

What does open awareness directed to the external world look like? Our older daughter, Hannah, practiced open awareness when she was one. We lived in a condo complex in a beige, concrete-covered part of Silicon Valley. Every morning, to get my nature-fix, I would carry Hannah around the labyrinthine paths of our development, winding among the manicured hedges and flower beds. Every ten feet or so Hannah would point and make a happy sound, and we would stop briefly at a leaf or a flower or even a pile of dog poo, whatever happened to capture her awareness. She would consider that thing for a moment. Then her interest would disengage, and we would move on to the next thing that might catch her awareness. She was noticing, releasing, repeating.

In some practices, the initial step of noticing may include lingering more extensively to name the thing or examine it a bit—but that isn't the point of practices that teach open awareness. Instead, open awareness, whether directed toward my interior world or my exterior world, always consists of a continuous flow that leads from briefly noticing to releasing and then to repeating that process.

In addition to intention and awareness, a third basic capacity shows up in spiritual practices: *attention*. Driving a car requires intention and broad, open awareness, but it also requires the ability to focus for an extended period—to notice something and to stay focused on it rather than to release it. If Monica had been unable to focus her attention on an upcoming traffic light, even as she was preoccupied with thoughts of the clutch or sightings of an iguana, she might have missed the fact that the light had turned red just as she reached it. Without a strong capacity for attention, she would not have been able to master the shifting challenges driving a manual car presents.

The same can be said for spiritual practices. For example, if I am singing an unfamiliar hymn, I must focus most of my attention on the words my mouth is forming. Otherwise, the song will fade on my lips, and I will lose the intention of the spiritual practice. Or if I am studying a Bible passage, I need to focus on the words to explore their meanings. Otherwise, I will lose my intention in the practice—to deepen my understanding of scripture.

At the compassion conference, my spy friend and I shared our stories in our first conversation. Then we allowed many memories to wash through our awareness, releasing them from our attention, focusing on none. During our second meeting, we focused our attention on a specific part of his story—his painful longing for a new life—and together we explored that longing and what it might mean for his future.

I've made a point to say that intention, awareness, and attention show up in every spiritual practice. But as I've suggested, that doesn't mean they have equal power in every practice; a specific practice may emphasize one or more of the foundational spiritual capacities. Two practices, one from Buddhism and one from Christianity, illustrate how this works.

In some versions of the Buddhist practice of *shamatha*, you might be invited to sit quietly and begin to focus your *attention* on your breath as it comes through your nostrils. Your intention is to maintain this quiet focus. At the point when you became aware that you were thinking of something other than your breath (that is, when your attention is drifting), you focus your attention back to your breath.

Notice how *shamatha* highlights attention. The honed stabilizing of attention is what's important. Intention and awareness are tools that help focus attention.

The second example is the single-word Christian meditation practice popularized by the Benedictine monk John Main.[7] As in *shamatha*, the intention of this meditative process is to keep attention focused on one particular thing. But here attention is not focused on the breath. Instead, it is focused on a sacred word, *maranatha*, which means "Come, Lord" in Aramaic. The word is meant to help you keep your entire being focused on Christ.

The process is simple: Gently repeat the word *maranatha*. When you become aware that you have stopped repeating it—that is, when your attention has drifted from the word—you turn your focus back to repeating it. Attention to the repetition of the word is the core activity of the practice. In Main's Christian meditation—as in Buddhist *shamatha*—intention and awareness serve as tools that help this attention remain focused and stable.

Other practices highlight awareness rather than attention. In Buddhism, a practice known as *vipassana* recognizes that your mind constantly generates thoughts, feelings, and images. These flow through your experience whether you like it or not. A version of *vipassana* might invite you to become quiet and focus on none of these inner movements. Instead, when you become aware that you have focused on something, you release it from your attention (there are many techniques for this) and return to an open awareness—a stance that gently notices whatever arises but hangs on to nothing. An intention of *vipassana* can be to gain deeper insight into the ever-changing nature of experience, life, and reality itself.

A second example of an awareness practice appears within the Christian Ignatian practice of the Awareness Examen. The first step of this practice (the "awareness" part) invites you to let your memory gently scan a set period, such as the previous twenty-four hours. This memory review involves focusing on nothing in particular. Instead it allows the events, encounters, and situations of the past day to emerge into your current awareness. The intention of this awareness exercise is to bring to the surface moments of experience that you may meditatively explore through a process of focused attention (the "Examen" part of the practice).

Even those Christian spiritual practices that highlight one capacity, whether intention, awareness, or attention, incorporate all three. In some form or other, these three Foundational Capacities show up in every spiritual practice (not to mention every waking human activity), including those that name the formation of compassion as a goal.[8]

When it comes to forming compassion, however, the Foundational Capacities need help. That is where the Compassion Capacities come in.

The Compassion Capacities: Intimacy, Imagination, and Feelings

Compassion Capacities are the special muscles needed in the building of compassion. They are *intimacy, imagination,* and *feelings.* Let's look at how these Compassion Capacities work.

The compassion capacity of *intimacy* refers to our ability to form deep, vulnerable relationships with others.[9] Recall my encounter with my spy friend. The first step in that compassion practice was an invitation to enter into an experience of intimacy. The leadership asked us to open our lives to each other and to be transparent. We told our stories and listened without critique or comment. This intimacy, a profound stance of presence toward each other, formed a safe, secure foundation for a new way of being to unfold.

Imagination encompasses the range of mental images, dreams, and fantasies that flow through our inner world. When my friend began to recall his marriage, his wife, and his child, he was intentionally using the capacity of imagination—in this case, images formed from his memories—to explore what was true and vital in his life. From those memory-images he began to imagine what his life might be like in the future if he had a different job. He began to dream of new possibilities, fashioning ideas about them and drawing mental pictures of them, trying on a new life for himself and his family.

Maybe you have done something similar, imagining yourself in a new setting, envisioning a new vocation, or picturing the person you would love to be with. Of course, depending on how you use it, the power of imagination can lead to fixations rather than freedom, obsessions rather than openings. For this reason, some Christian spiritual practices discourage using the imagination. But compassion practices embrace it. They show us how to harness the power of imagination for enlivening our selves, our relationships, and our service in the world.

Feelings covers the wide range of emotions we experience in relation to the many movements of daily life.[10] At the reconciliation conference, my spy friend and I were brought to tears by his plight and his longings. Our feelings cracked open our shells of fearful posturing so that we recognized and responded to the truth, the divine humanity, in each other. Because feelings are so powerful, certain traditions of spiritual practice avoid them altogether, convinced they are dangerous.

Other practice traditions take a second approach. They try to ignore or stamp out so-called "negative" feelings (such as fear, anger, and jealousy), while they encourage those they see as "positive" (including joy, gratitude, and empathy). Many of the historical compassion practices we will explore take this route.

Still other practices follow a third and ultimately more helpful path for forming compassion. They treat all feelings, whether positive or negative, as fertile soil for growing compassion. This approach combines ancient spiritual wisdom with current neuroscientific understandings of emotion.[11] In the chapter on the Compassion Practice, we will explore how all our emotions are vital for forming compassion. But for now, it is enough to emphasize that over the ages Christian compassion practices intentionally draw on the power of at least some feelings.

Christianity is not the only spiritual tradition that highlights intimacy, imagination, and feelings in compassion practices. They appear, for example, in a 1,100-year-old Tibetan Buddhist compassion meditation called "Sevenfold Cause and Effect."[12] This practice invites you to recall that all beings are *intimately* connected to you since (according to this tradition's understandings of reincarnation) every one of them has been your mother. Then you use your *imagination* to experience what it feels like (the *feelings* now become involved) to be intimately loved as a child by your mother. You also imagine what it feels like to experience suffering in the absence of such love. These feelings create the desire for other persons' suffering to be relieved—not only people close to you but also those more distant and even enemies.

Over the ages, the folks who have engaged in compassion practices—whether in Buddhism, Christianity, or other traditions—have carefully tended intimacy, imagination, and feelings. In the process, these practitioners have become more familiar with their interior world, its ebb and flow, its actions and reactions, and the dynamics that enliven it and deaden it. Noticing, exploring, and nurturing these capacities really can grow compassion. Understanding how the Compassion Capacities function can help us enter or teach them more easily. So, I will be inviting you to call upon the Compassion Capacities with each of the compassion practices in which we engage.

I encourage you not to get hung up by specific exercises, processes, or technical details within our exploration of the practices. Use these teaching devices only to the extent that they help grow compassion in your life. Remember, growing compassion is the point.

Recall when I was rocking Monica. In those moments, long before I had even begun to consider spiritual capacities or compassion practices, I experienced compassion: I profoundly connected with Monica and with Divine Presence (as *intimacy* deepening); I felt deep care flowing to and through me (as my *feelings* expanding); I envisioned myself held in loving arms (as my *imagination* enlivening). As I recall those moments, I

trust that your life too has been graced with a compassion that knows
no bounds.

Review and Practice

In this chapter, we moved from a rocking chair to a Volvo, detoured
through a violence-torn land, visited a few spiritual practices from both
Christianity and Buddhism, and returned to the rocking chair. Along
the way, some key understandings of the Christian version of compassion have come into focus:

- Genuine compassion encompasses understandings, feelings,
  actions, wisdom, and restoration.
- Compassion is grounded in an experience of receiving compassion from the eternal Source of Compassion.
- Fullness of compassion for others requires compassion for yourself, and vice versa.

In addition, we have touched on the tending of certain spiritual
capacities within compassion practices:

- By honing the Foundational Capacities of *intention, attention,*
  and *awareness*, we form a base for compassion.
- By harnessing the power of the Compassion Capacities—*intimacy, imagination,* and *feelings*—we build compassion in our
  lives.

Exercises for the Spiritual Capacities

The following exercises offer simple ways to hone the six spiritual capacities for forming compassion. ("Exercises" refers to movements drawn
from spiritual "practices," which are processes that are richer and more
multidimensional than typical exercises.[13])

Feel free to prepare to enter these exercises (and any other exercises
and practices I present) in whatever way is most familiar and comfortable. If you do not have a process for centering or grounding yourself, see
the "Review and Practice" section at the end of chapter 2 for possibilities.

I encourage you to take the exercises and practices seriously and carry them lightly. Receive them as processes for you to try on, work with, and explore in whatever way may benefit the expansion of compassion in your life.

Exercises for the Foundational Capacities: Intention, Awareness, and Attention

The first exercise highlights *attention* to a movement in your body, as well as the *intention* to remain focused on that movement. The second exercise highlights open *awareness* of whatever may come into your experience, as well as the *intention* to maintain this awareness.

An Exercise That Engages "Attention with Intention" (5-20 Minutes)

- Sit in a comfortable position.
- Draw your attention to your diaphragm rising and falling with the natural movement of your breathing. As you do this, silently name your intention: *I will keep my attention focused on the movement of my breathing.*
- Whenever you notice that you are not focused on the movement of your breathing, remind yourself of your intention.
- Turn your attention back to the movement of your breathing.

An Exercise That Engages "Awareness with Intention" (5-20 Minutes)

- Find a comfortable position that you can hold easily for an extended time. Silently name your intention: *I will simply be here, in open awareness.*
- Just be there, sitting without trying to do or be anything. Do not focus your thoughts or attention on anything.

- After some moments, you may notice that your attention is drawn to something around you or within you. (Do you begin to hear the smallest sound? Do thoughts about lunch or the meeting tomorrow or any other matters come up? Do feelings arise? How about mental pictures?)
- Silently name what you notice; briefly describe it as an event outside yourself, even if it is within you. (For example: *There is a thought about the tangerine I ate for breakfast.*)
- After you have named the thought, release it from your attention and return to simply being there, open, focused on nothing in particular.
- Repeat the process with the next thing you notice.

An Exercise for the Compassion Capacities: Imagination, Intimacy, and Feelings

- Sit in a comfortable position.
- Call to your memory a time when someone you cared about gave you a special gift. Perhaps it was a surprise, or maybe it was during a holiday or for a special occasion.
- In any case, let yourself relive the event you are picturing in your memory, that moment of seeing it, realizing who gave it to you, your gratitude, your feeling of your close relationship with this person you cared about, what this person said or did, what you said or did in response to the gift.
- Take a few moments and settle into that memory.
- After some moments, notice what you were feeling at the time.
- Notice what you are feeling as you relive the moment.

Notice how this brief exercise uses the Compassion Capacities. *Intimacy* shows up when you focus your memory on "a close relationship with someone you cared about." *Imagination* appears when you "relive the event you are picturing in your memory." *Feelings* are in play whenever you focus on an emotion.

As we'll see when we begin looking at compassion practices, the Compassion Capacities play off of and intensify one another. For example, once imagination is active, feelings and images begin to flourish. In the above exercise, it would be difficult to imagine yourself into that memory without reliving in the present some version of what you felt and saw in the past. In fact, this cascading, intertwining effect is what seems to make the Compassion Capacities so powerfully transformative.

CHAPTER 2

Compassion Practices for Grounding in Divine Presence

Not long ago my wife Steffani and our friend Ron were walking a dusty fire road along the Sacramento River. It was late morning, and they were taking a short break from a conference they were attending. As they walked, they chatted about the conference presentations, their families, and whatever else came to mind. Then in an instant three things happened: a six-foot rattlesnake hurled toward them; Steffani leapt into the air with a scream; Ron stiffened, immobilized, glued to his spot in the dust.

You can imagine the possible outcomes of this once-peaceful stroll. Thankfully, no one was hurt, so we are free to look at what was happening with each player in this spontaneous drama. Their responses sprang from a gift found in perhaps all living creatures: the automatic reaction to preserve life. This life-saving auto-reactivity takes many forms.

For instance, the snake, sensing it might be stepped on, exploded into fight mode, automatically going on the offensive. It attacked the threat before it was too late to defend itself from harm.

Steffani, on the other hand, automatically launched into flight mode. She ended up more than fifteen feet from her lift-off point, her body moving toward safety before she was even conscious a snake was nearby.

Ron went into freeze mode. His body automatically assessed that, by remaining completely motionless, it could avoid attracting danger.

All of these reactions—fight, flight, and freeze—were immediate, spontaneous, and meant to save the body that carried it. In many animals, including humans, this fight-flight-freeze reaction happens not only for self-preservation but also to protect others.[1]

Scientists tell us that these reactions, these life-preserving gifts, are made up of a string of automatic neurophysiological processes.[2] For instance, on that trail along the river, a snake-shaped chunk of light and shadow reached the neurons in Steffani's brain, which triggered a rush of chemicals, including adrenaline, that threw her leg muscles into hyperdrive—all before her intellect knew there was a problem. In and of itself this super-powered chain of reactions is a blessing, a gift from how we are constructed; it helps us stay alive in life-threatening emergencies.

But these life-saving chains of reactivity can also harm our lives. They can hurt our bodies and our relationships.

First, let's look at what happens in our bodies. During the fight-flight-freeze reaction, the neurochemical rush provides the power. This rush is both a blessing and a curse.

An example from the automobile world reveals how this blessing-with-a-curse works. If a driver runs a red light and races toward you, you can tromp the accelerator in your vehicle, which rushes fuel to its engine and moves you out of harm's way. But mechanics (and your parents, if you were ever the speed-obsessed teenager of my own youth) will tell you that each jackrabbit start damages your car's internal workings a bit. If you tromp the accelerator whenever you leave an intersection, tires and engine parts will give out before their intended time. Yes, that constant rush of fuel is helpful in the right situations—but it is toxic if used habitually. (Monica was thrilled to have me share this bit of wisdom with her in our driving lessons.)

Just as jackrabbit starts harm cars, the neurochemicals that fuel our fight-flight-freeze reactions can wear out our bodies. Our bodies can take periodic doses of these chemicals and even require them in special situations, like dodging rattlesnakes for example. But doses delivered repeatedly over time destroy our bodies because the neurochemicals themselves are toxins. They make our bodies work harder and wear them down more quickly.

Since we don't face fight-flight-freeze situations constantly, we assume that we function mostly free of these toxic floods. But we assume incorrectly. Any time we feel stressed or anxious, fight-flight-freeze neurochemicals flow through us, causing our bodies to remain in high gear, as if we are reacting to that "rattlesnake" in our path. The snake might be the job interview, the driver's test, the bank overdraft, the deadlines that are piling up with no time to meet them. The dominant culture in North America, with its pace and expectations, is tailor-made to create constant stress in our lives and to keep those protective fight-flight-freeze neurochemicals always flowing and poisoning our bodies.

Our bodies are not the only things that a surplus of this protective gift can poison. The fight-flight-freeze reaction can also poison relationships. For example, a colleague unsuspectingly taps into my insecurities by offering a critique of my presentation at a faculty meeting, and *I* become the rattlesnake: verbal attack launched, *fight* mode fully activated. My sister teases me in a way that brings up childhood pains, and suddenly she's the attacking rattlesnake: I avoid her for a month, my protective neurochemicals sending me into *flight* mode. Or two aggressively arguing friends turn suddenly to me for my opinion on the matter (which of course I have), and I'm tongue-tied, terrified that my slightest sound will turn their aggression toward me: *freeze* reaction engaged.

Anything my physical sensations, conscious awareness, unconscious awareness, body memory, or psychological sensibilities register as a potential threat activates the fight-flight-freeze rush—which we'll call the *3F state*. In the 3F state, our Divine gift of self-preservation can turn into a defensive weapon that harms relationships.

Experts from many fields have begun focusing on the challenges of the 3F state. Some have addressed 3F-generated health problems with a variety of medications, including anti-anxiety drugs and sleep aids. Countless books, seminars, courses, and life coaches have offered techniques and tools for improving interpersonal relationships. In addition, medical and psychological researchers have recently turned their sights toward the ancient spiritual practices of religious traditions.

These researchers are finding that certain spiritual practices mitigate, ease, or regulate this automatic reactivity.[3] Regularly engaging in these spiritual practices changes our neurophysiological makeup so that we become less reactive to the world around us. That is, instead of being only reactive, we are freed to be *appropriately responsive*. Even our automatic reactions will match the needs of the situation more closely. We will leap automatically out of the way of striking rattlesnakes, rather than meditatively letting them bite us. We will calmly respond to the stresses of modern life, rather than letting them poison us with stress. We will creatively imagine possibilities for new ways of being and acting, rather than freezing in confusion. Our minds and bodies can be released from the damaging consequences of unrelenting 3F states.

Spiritual sages throughout the centuries and across traditions have understood these practices long before scientific research confirmed them. Spiritual teachers developed their knowledge through observing what happened when they and others prayed, experimenting with different ways of praying and mentoring one another in what they learned.

Fortunately, the medical and mental health-care professionals who offer practices drawn from spiritual traditions have recognized how helpful they can be as alternatives to medication, extensive individual and interpersonal therapy, or expensive and invasive surgical procedures. To make these practices and their benefits as accessible as possible, the health-care world has downplayed their roots in religious traditions.

Some religious leaders have encouraged this approach, as they recognize the value of making the benefits of the practices as widely available as possible. For example, His Holiness the Dalai Lama continually invites people to find ways to strip Buddhist meditative practices of the language and concepts that make them *Buddhist* so that all people may more easily enjoy their benefits.

I want to be clear: I believe it is vital that the health and well-being community members continue to develop and promote meditative practices that provide medical and psychological benefits to meet the needs of more people. The Dalai Lama is right to encourage efforts to develop practices derived from Buddhist meditation but stripped of Buddhist language and concepts. At the same time, I value the uniqueness that religious traditions bring to the spiritual practices that are the foundation of many of today's popular meditative practices. I believe that while something is gained within the practices when they are removed from their spiritual tradition, something is also lost—including particular perspectives on life, ethical behaviors, and the world that are important to the faithful followers of the traditions that developed the practices in the first place.[4] Spiritual practices can be more powerful for us as we understand more fully how they connect with the traditions that created them. What is lost—for better and for worse—when we separate a practice from its tradition? And when we hold the tradition close, what is added?

Christian tradition has an answer to questions of what is lost or added: God. But what does that mean for what happens within a practice? What benefit does the God-element add within the practice itself? I'm not talking here about cosmic benefits that may or may not relate to spiritual practices—eternal life, for example. I'll leave those questions for all of us to work out in our own fear and trembling. Instead, I'm talking about what goes on in a practice. Many Christian practices, as we will see, use rhythmic breathing, relaxation processes, focused attention, and open awareness in ways that ease the rush of 3F neurochemicals just as "secularized" meditative practices do. But when we consider God, what does God add to these practices?

Christian practices, including the ones explicitly focused on forming compassion, encourage above all connecting with a Divine Presence and settling into a feeling of being in relationship with an Eternal Source of Compassion. With this feeling of relationship comes a sense of receiving compassion from Eternal Compassion. From a neurophysiological perspective, this experience of receiving compassion through resting in the Source of Compassion grounds the body and mind by easing the rush of 3F neurochemicals, short-circuiting reactivity. Neuropsychologist Rick Hanson calls this the "Rest and Digest" state.[5]

This Compassion-grounded, "Rest and Digest" state can set us on a path to physical and mental well-being. However, Christian spiritual traditions insist the purpose is something other than personal well-being. Being in intimate relationship with God, the Eternal Source of Compassion, is both the means and the end: We are invited to ground ourselves in Divine Compassion, receive Compassion, become filled with the Presence of Compassion, so that we become images of God, living expressions of the Eternal Source of Compassion.

This relationship makes sense to me as I recall my moments of holding baby Monica, rocking her, and feeling God's love flow in and through me. The power of connecting to a Loving Other greater than myself has been verified by studies of how babies attach to their mothers. Humans fail to thrive—both physically and emotionally—if they have no positive relationship with someone who gives them loving, appropriate care. In that situation, babies live in a perpetual state of high alert, ready to fight, flee, or freeze, poisoning their bodies over the long term.

When we receive love and care, the core of our beings, the soul of who we are, even our neurophysiological structure, carries a divine gift: the ability to be comforted, stilled, calmed, grounded, and strengthened through the experience of receiving compassion from a compassionate Presence we know is *for* us.[6]

Grounding in Compassion Takes Practice

Many years ago, I spent a year living as a volunteer at a monastic community. My inner life was in turmoil at the time; the brothers were very kind to take me on. The monk who was my spiritual director, Brother Matthew, was gracious given how cranky I was.

Matthew was a bespectacled, compact, calm man in his forties. He'd been an Irish pastor before running off and joining the monastery. That had been twenty-odd years before, but his Irish brogue remained. One of Matthew's signature techniques during spiritual direction was to fill extended, reflective pauses with long, slow breaths, inhaling and exhaling—before he voiced the words of wisdom all his advisees had come to expect of him.

One time in a spiritual-direction meeting with Brother Matthew, about two months into my stay, I was complaining about something, as usual. This time it had to do with life at the monastery. I explained that I didn't like the work I'd been assigned, and how frustrating it was that I was never even told what work I'd be doing each week until the week began, and how annoying some of the volunteers were, and how the food was not that great, and that I was not thrilled to be sharing a room with someone, and as a matter of fact, "If it weren't for the communal prayers three times a day, I wouldn't even stay here."

As Brother Matthew took his famous meditative breaths, I pondered how much I had come to love the silence, chants, and sense of secure rest the monastic prayers gave me during the otherwise mundane and repetitious schedule that was the bane of my existence. Then Brother Matthew's long exhaling ended, and he asked, "So you wouldn't stay if it weren't for the prayers?" "Nope. Not a chance," I said. His response: "Well, *none* of us would, you know."

Ah, I get it.

The brothers had committed themselves to lives devoted solely to focusing on God. But every moment wasn't a divine revelry for them—any more than it was for me. They had to work and eat and live together and figure out how to negotiate all the petty, annoying nuisances of daily life just as I did. But they knew something I didn't. They had something I hadn't: the daily office, the communal prayer. Three times every day for their entire lives they filed to the church and sat and stood in silence and song and scripture. They needed that prayer. It was the steady heartbeat of their community. That spiritual practice was what grounded their lives in Divine Compassion. Without that grounding, none of the monks would have stayed.

Daily communal prayer is not the only grounding practice in Christianity. The tradition has many spiritual practices for grounding in Divine Compassion. Each of them creates the starting point, the foundation, and the abiding stability for forming compassionate lives. We will explore three examples, each of which offers its own unique approach to grounding in Compassion.

The first practice is a prayer practice that may have developed within the first 350 years of Christianity. It arose among the desert monastics in the Middle East and North Africa as they sought to "pray without ceasing."

The second practice comes to us from the sixteenth-century writings of Teresa of Avila. It is a version of the practice known as Recollection.

The third practice, Centering Prayer, took shape toward the end of the twentieth century. It's an updated version of a practice described in a writing from the fourteenth century.

From the Desert: Praying Without Ceasing

Christian understandings of compassion are rooted in scripture. The same is true of Christian practices that form compassion, even though scripture has no prescribed formula for developing compassion. The biblical background for Christian compassion practices derives from a statement in one of Paul's letters: "Pray without ceasing" (1 Thess. 5:17).

Paul doesn't say how to pray without ceasing. But certain early Christians took his words at face value, seeing them as a command to practice a way of praying that eventually took many forms, including those that focused on forming compassion.

The prayer was meant to calm, center, strengthen, and steady the soul and to alleviate fear and distress. In physiological terms, the prayer draws us to a "rest and digest" state, the opposite of the 3F state. The desert tradition knew nothing of twenty-first-century neurophysiology. For the desert monastics who developed the prayer, God was always the key ingredient. For them, the calming, centering, strengthening effects of their unceasing prayer resulted from their grounding in Divine Compassion. This unceasing prayer from the desert is the oldest known formalized version of a Christian spiritual practice meant to ground us in the Divine Presence that is Compassion.[7]

What was the form of this unceasing prayer? And how did it develop? To answer that, I ask you to indulge the spirituality professor within me as I offer a brief history lesson. I've found that understanding the context of the practice can help in the understanding of the practice itself.

Christianity in the fourth century was gaining power both politically and culturally. The emperor had all but declared it to be the state religion. Government leaders were embracing it. Clergy were moving from being vilified to valued. Christianity's stock was rising. But some Christians thought this acceptance was a bad thing. They saw Christianity as selling out to secular powers and cultural trends. They believed it was being co-opted by the government to increase rulers' power over the people. They insisted that when the church and the state work together, faith gets watered down, and the state wins.

This church-state collusion significantly reversed the existing situation. In the first three centuries of Christianity, Christians were killed by the Roman forces because of their faith. With this persecution came a strong sense among many Christians that martyrdom and faith went hand in hand. To remain true to God's way, one had to be willing to sacrifice much. In the time before the emperor Constantine embraced Christianity, the Christian's sacrifice could include life itself. After Christianity became the dominant religion, government forces no longer threatened Christians' lives because of their faith. Christians who were inclined toward a heroic faith had to look for other ways to sacrifice, to be martyrs. For some, going to the desert to be alone satisfied this urge. It was a "little martyrdom," the sacrifice of a comfortable, urban lifestyle for endless wilderness camping.

Have you ever been alone in the wilderness? If so, maybe you have had a small taste of what the desert sages might have experienced. I think the closest I have come to that was during a trip to the vast desert of southern Jordan, an area called Wadi Rum, a few miles from Saudi Arabia. The old movie *Lawrence of Arabia* and the recent film *The Martian* were set in Wadi Rum—the former because that's where Lawrence actually did the things he was famous for and the latter because the landscape looks like Mars. Wadi Rum is miles and miles of windswept sand dunes and scorched, fortress-sized rocks.

My trip was meant to be less dramatic than the ones in the movies. I decided to spend a night camping in the desert, a tame tourist adventure arranged by residents of the area to help sustain their local economy. My camping trip began with a patient young Bedouin guide leading me through the desert for a day—by jeep, on foot, and on the back of a camel. The stark beauty held me spellbound. I felt completely at ease in the care of my guide.

I enjoyed myself until about halfway through the day, many miles into the heart of the dunes. There, just after the hottest part of the afternoon, which we spent picnicking and napping in the shade of a massive rock, my guide stopped his jeep and invited me to hop out. I did. He gestured toward a huge cleft in a rock mesa and explained that if I walked into the shadowed, sandy canyon formed by that cleft, he would meet me "at the other end" in an hour or so. "I will leave you here," he said. And he drove away before I could speak.

As I watched the jeep disappear into the proverbial cloud of dust, terrifying thoughts began to grow in me: *What if I get lost? . . . What if my guide arrived too early? Or too late? Or didn't show up at all? . . . Surely I have cell service. . . . Of course not! I'm in the middle of nowhere. Where I am defines "nowhere!" . . . Do I have enough water? What about food? . . . What kinds of animals live in desert rocks? Can I eat them? Can they eat me? . . .* In a sci-fi book series I read as a teenager, giant worm-things come out of the sand and swallow every creature in sight. *Does Wadi Rum have giant worm-things? If I feed them my protein bars, will that be enough? Or should I save those for later? Maybe I can put one in the sand for the worm-things and keep the rest for myself until I'm rescued. If I'm rescued.* And that was only the first five minutes. The 3Fs grew and grew in me. Eventually, my imagination saw the giant worm-things chasing me through moonless darkness as I threw pieces of protein bar into the sand to entice the worms, who might, I could only hope, be health-conscious vegetarians.

At this point I'd like to tell you all about the huge, attacking, worm-like things I heroically fought off before dragging myself through the sand to meet my guide, but the worms never showed up. Everything turned out okay for me in Wadi Rum. I had only to trust my guide, who met me as he had said he would. I spent a wonderful night in a cozy tent in the desert. And I gained some sense of what the early desert sages might have experienced in the unfamiliar solitude of the wilderness.

The ancient monastics describe fears of the unknown that constantly grew in them. They faced and fought the "demons" of loneliness, hunger, thirst, and real and imagined creatures every bit as terrifying as my giant worm-things. In the desert, these ancient sages felt attacked from all sides. All the conveniences and comforts of the city, the companionship of friends, and support of family were gone. They were left alone with themselves, their own thoughts, fantasies, and desires. That was no surprise. They had come to the desert to escape distractions so that they could directly face the roots of their fears, uncertainties, and temptations and make themselves fully available to God. They knew that during their solitary struggles, their only recourse was to trust the Divine Guide who would always point the true way through their desert, never abandoning them, keeping them safe day and night.

How did the desert sages maintain their trust in God? How did they remain calm, focused, and clear, warding off overwhelming 3F states? They developed a practice that followed Paul's invitation to "pray constantly." They borrowed words from the scriptures that they had memorized: "Be pleased, O God, to deliver me. O LORD, make haste to help me!" (Ps. 70:1)[8]

This verse became a mantra for the monks. They believed the words embraced "all the feelings which can be implanted in human nature, and can be fitly and satisfactorily adapted to every condition, and all assaults."[9] The prayer expressed 1) faith that God was present; 2) trust that the pray-er would not be abandoned to wild animals and destructive inner voices; 3) the humility of knowing human limitations; 4) intense desire for intimate connection with God; and 5) awe and adoration in the face of God's all-compassionate immensity. In fact, the desert sages believed that this prayer covers every dimension of human life, whatever comes up in a person's thoughts and feelings and in the world. It serves every purpose in every time. To this day, the words of this mantra open monastic prayer services.[10]

On the surface, this prayer may not seem like a compassion practice. However, it sets the stage for the heart of compassion-forming practices in Christianity (and for all other prayer practices too). Why? Because the process invites us to call upon Divine Presence and to turn and open our entire beings to that Presence. In that turning and opening, we allow ourselves to experience all the compassion God offers, an essential part of Christian spiritual practices.

Recall the three dimensions of Christian compassion formation: a sense of grounding in Divine Compassion, compassion for oneself, and compassion for another. Without the first, the other two cannot flourish. The desert sages knew that. I learned that from my spiritual-director monk, Brother Matthew: Without continuous grounding in Divine Compassion, the life of compassion we long for will never come into being.

The desert sages sought to ground themselves in Divine Compassion when they experienced fear, anguish, sadness, despair, and longings— and from all other conceivable emotional states. They called upon God, trusting that the compassion of God would surround them with safety, strength, and fearless calm. These sages knew that before we can offer full compassion to others, we must begin settling into this sense of endless strength, safety, and calm. This deep connection satisfies a fundamental need in human life. We cannot thrive without it.

Neuroscientists consider this need for connection to be a part of the basic biological instincts all mammals—including humans—have for caring relationships. Psychologists relate it to the need for secure attachment, a trustworthy grounding in the love of a sensitive, responsive caregiver.[11] Christian spiritual practice traditions view it as the indispensable heart of a life of love, a life of compassion. To love, we need to be held in Love. To offer compassion, we need to receive the Presence of Compassion; we need to be grounded in Compassion.

The process of being grounded in Compassion, resting in Love, is the beginning point and abiding core of every compassion practice in the Christian traditions. This grounding in Compassion stabilizes and calms us amid whatever wilderness struggles we may find ourselves. Maybe the wilderness struggles are the wild creations of an anxiety-fueled imagination, like those giant worm-things pursuing me in the sands of the Jordanian desert. Or maybe they are the shattering spiritual, psychological, and physical turmoils of seeking an authentic life with God, like those ancient Christian sages constantly repeating psalms in their desert hermitages. Or maybe the wilderness struggles come in simple attempts to follow God's invitations within the ordinary moments of our daily routines. Without grounding in the Presence of Compassion, any fears, anxieties, tensions, and other reactivities that circle within us can overwhelm us, locking us into 3F states that throw us off the path we long to travel. But with it, we can be open and available to have Compassion fill and shape our lives. Grounding in the Presence of Compassion forms a foundation on which we can build compassionate lives.

Teresa of Avila's "Recollection"

The ancient desert hermits developed their own way of grounding in Divine Compassion, a way that helped them stay steady, anchored in the peace and courage of God, even in their isolated wilderness. A thousand years later, a sixteenth-century Spanish activist-mystic-nun, Saint Teresa of Avila, offered another way of grounding in Compassion. She and many others in her tradition called this Recollection. Historians know quite a bit about Teresa's life and thought.[12] But there's something I've always suspected they've missed: Saint Teresa was a junior-high youth-group leader. Surely this is true; you can see it in her Recollection practice. Let me explain.

During the twenty years I worked as a pastor in small churches, I was usually the staff member who worked with the junior-high youth groups. I consider those groups the Mount Everest of ministry challenges. I valued those groups. I formed them. I argued for their preservation. I developed curricula and practices for them. And I gathered adult leaders to help me guide them. I fervently believe these groups are vital to the heart of the church.

Still, every Sunday evening as youth-group time approached, fear and trembling settled over me. I fantasized about being ill or called to a pastoral emergency—anything to avoid facing that terrifying body of uncontrollable energy. Week after week I was barely able to tame my flight instincts. Time and again I willed myself to fulfill my youth-leader responsibilities, only to stand clueless before those highly energetic young people, unable to come up with any strategy that channeled their energy in constructive, helpful ways. They might as well have been a room full of wildcats for all the control I had over them: wrestling, rolling, snarling, howling, tumbling, leaping, darting, batting at one another and at me.

This happened again and again, Sunday after Sunday, and I muddled through. It wasn't until years later that my friend Mark Yaconelli helped me see what these meetings were trying to teach me about *my* spiritual life: My youth groups were a metaphor for my own inner world. The way I related to them was like the way I relate to the random feelings, thoughts, fantasies, memories, images, and mental conversations constantly flowing through my mind. They scurry and leap and rush around, and I want to flee from them, or I freeze in their presence, or sometimes I even fight them as I argue and cajole, trying to be the controlling, containing authority. I want them to stop, to be subdued by me, to go away, or in some other way to give me some peace. Instead, there they are, full of energy, irrepressible, always with me, a perpetual junior-high youth group inside my head. And this "monkey mind" activity (as

Buddhist traditions call it) keeps the 3F toxins flowing freely through my body constantly. There is no escape from that junior-high group inside my head. I can't go home after the meeting ends. All that inner activity, sometimes frantic, sometimes distracting, can exhaust me in the short term and harm me in the long term.

How do I deal with an untamed mind? This is where Teresa of Avila comes in. Okay, I admit that she wasn't a junior-high youth-group leader. But her Recollection practice is tailor-made to address *inner* junior-high youth groups, just like the one that inhabits my head. Her writings tell of her personal spiritual struggles by describing in detail the dynamic feelings and thoughts of her interior world. Teresa's practice of Recollection helped her stay grounded in Divine Compassion even as she experienced inner turmoil connected to her efforts to restore her religious order.

Recollection addresses that interior turmoil, the stream of inner activity, by focusing attention toward God. Draw your attention into yourself so that you are focused on God alone, says Teresa. Attend to God's presence within you and with you, and attend to your presence before God.[13]

Teresa uses several images to help us in this process. In the first image she describes a person—a soul—as being like a castle. At the center of the castle is the King, God. The people of the castle are all the pieces of a person's internal life: thoughts, emotions, longings, intentions, imaginings, fantasies, and physical sensations. Teresa, true to her time, called these *faculties*. Others have called them *energies* or *interior movements*. For me, these energetic inner movements are like the members of a junior-high youth group, scattered and unfocused.

In Teresa's castle metaphor, interior movements are like crowds of people outside the castle walls, going about their business, scattered around the city. But it's possible for them to gather inside the castle and focus together on being with the king and at the service of the king.

Teresa also describes Recollection as being like a turtle drawing into its shell, gathering itself into its core; or like a hedgehog curling up, drawing into itself in stillness and security.[14] No matter what metaphor Teresa uses, her point is clear: All these energetic movements, rather than being scattered to various attentions, are now focused on one thing, open to one thing, settling into one thing, grounding in one thing—the Compassionate Presence at the heart of it all.

I think of Recollection when I call a class together to begin a discussion, and I think of it during the gathering moments and welcome time of worship services. I think of it in terms of those rare times when somehow, wondrously, my youth-group kids suddenly (no thanks to me) became completely focused on one thing, together. Perhaps it was a question someone asked or a mission-trip possibility raised or simply some random shared interest. In each of these cases, disparate energies—scattered, moving at cross-purposes or in unrelated directions—turn as one to a shared focus.

That is what Recollection does with all the movements that populate my inner world: It brings them to a shared focus. One contemporary writer sees this focus having two dimensions that together play off the dual meaning of the Spanish word (recogimento) that Teresa used for the practice: (1) a re-collecting—bringing the movements and parts and functions of ourselves into some semblance of order and focus; and (2) a remembering—remembering who and what lie beneath and within and around our lives.[15]

Versions of this process appear throughout the Christian spiritual-practice traditions. For instance, can you see how the desert mantra prayer was a form of Recollection, even though the sages did not give it that name? The desert hermits used their scriptural mantra to center themselves, still themselves, and ground themselves in God. Through heartfelt repetition of words, they received the Divine Compassion that constantly flowed to them.

Centuries later and worlds away, Teresa's form of Recollection offered a different way: She encouraged her sisters to look upon Divine images rather than repeat words as the desert sages did. For her, sight and pictures, not speech and words, offer the more powerful path. Teresa describes how visual images most fully help us "recollect our outward senses . . . and give them something which will occupy them" so that we can be present to God.[16] First, she invites us to form a mental picture of Jesus or to find an actual picture of him. Then she says, "I am asking you only to look at him." Look at Christ not only with your physical eyes or your imagination but also with the "eyes of your soul." There's no need to think heady thoughts about who Jesus is or what Christ means "or to make long and subtle meditations with your understanding." Instead, simply gaze upon the One who holds you in love. In whatever state you are, look upon Jesus. Look upon Jesus in all times, whether in times of sadness, joy, fear, or pain. Notice that Jesus, in turn, looks upon you.[17]

Teresa calls this process of mutual gazing a "holy companionship."[18] This companionship is a circle of compassion, a mutual giving and receiving. When you look at Jesus suffering the pain of the cross, you will see that Jesus looks upon you with "compassionate eyes," longing to comfort your grief. Surrounded by this Divine Compassion, you will offer Jesus "the compassion of your heart," longing to comfort his suffering.[19] She says to engage in this looking again and again, to let it form you over time.

Notice how Teresa's Recollection practice is really a kind of internal compassion practice. Seeing Jesus' compassion for us helps us receive and rest in Divine Compassion, and seeing Jesus' pain sparks our innate impulse for compassion. As this process happens repeatedly, grounding us in Compassion, it trains us to be compassionate. It stretches and exercises our compassion muscle so that it becomes flexible and strong.

In Teresa's spiritual practices, the compassion-training regimen takes place in the imagination, which carries impressive power. Neurophysiologists have shown that practicing something in our imagination increases our ability to act it out, explaining why elite athletes hire sports psychologists to help them imagine making the shot or nailing the landing. Acting something out over and over is the best practice, but imagination cultivates and waters the abilities that physical action grows.

In the practice of Recollection, as in the desert practice of praying without ceasing, we gather every part of our beings into an experience of Divine Presence, grounded in the Love that is God. The desert sages found attention to heartfelt *words* to be the avenue for receiving Compassion.

Teresa focused her attention on *images* of the soul's desire. Centuries later, a practice arose that drew on another pathway for grounding in Divine Compassion: Centering Prayer.

Centering Prayer

Some years ago, my friend Kay went on a weeklong silent retreat. No talking was allowed—except during her daily meetings with her spiritual director. At the end of her first meeting with him, he gave her an assignment: go contemplate a tree. So off she went to locate a tree. She found a stately maple. For the rest of that day and halfway through the next, she sat and examined that tree.

Then she met again with her spiritual director. "Tell me what you discovered," he said. Kay described how the roots of that tree anchored it into the ground, made it firm and strong, and how seeing that strong grounding, she was invited to dedicate herself to being anchored solidly in God's love. Kay's spiritual director looked at her in silence for a time. Then he said, "Go contemplate the tree."

Back Kay went to that maple. Again she examined it, explored its every crease and color, hours upon end, until it was time to return to her spiritual director: "Tell me what you discovered." Kay described how she noticed the branches reaching to the sky, like arms uplifted in praise and thanksgiving for all the rain and sun and all that kept it alive—and how seeing those expansive branches she was invited to live in gratitude to God for all the blessings she enjoyed in her life. Kay's spiritual director looked at her in silence. Then he said, "Go contemplate the tree."

Off Kay went, this time in rising frustration. She examined that maple again, hour after hour, until she sat before her spiritual director again, hearing once more, "Tell me what you discovered." "Leaves!" she said, her voice rising. "I discovered leaves! Beautiful leaves! And they reminded me of all the beautiful things I have to offer the world because of God's love!" Silence. And then, "Go contemplate the tree."

This time Kay virtually stormed to that maple. She threw herself down in front of it, tired of trying to understand what she was supposed to understand. She decided to just be there, thinking no thoughts about the tree, imagining nothing about what it might mean, examining nothing, exploring nothing—just waiting until her next spiritual-direction meeting. In that meeting, she once again heard those maddening words: "Tell me what you discovered." And Kay lost it: "IT'S A TREE!!!"

"Yes! That's it!" said her spiritual director. "It's a tree!" At that moment, Kay understood: All her spiritual director was asking her to do was simply to be there, to simply intend to remain open and available to whatever would come, without preconceptions or expectations, and without explorations or examinations—simply available.

Kay told me that story as we were trying to understand what it meant to practice one of the most widely recognized Christian contemplative practices among North American Christians: Centering Prayer. Centering Prayer isn't about thinking a certain thing or exploring a feeling or examining a metaphor that comes to mind or pondering an idea that comes to me or paying attention to anything in particular. It's about being available to the Presence of Compassion. Kay finally realized that all her spiritual director was asking her to do was bring herself to her tree and, once there, to be open and available. Centering Prayer invites us to bring ourselves to God and to be there, open and available.

Chances are that if you have engaged in a Christian contemplative practice, it will be Centering Prayer; it is probably the most well-known contemplative practice in mainstream Christianity. It is also one of the newest contemplative practices, though its roots are ancient. People who are already familiar with it may not think of Centering Prayer as a compassion practice. But according to Basil Pennington—one of the founders of Centering Prayer—the practice is a "school of compassion." Its fruits "can be summed up in one word: compassion." As we repeatedly engage in the prayer, says Pennington, "We become compassionate persons who feel with, are with, in a sensitive and sensing presence with reality, with God, with . . . creation, with other persons, with our own true selves."[20]

How does this compassion formation happen? What is it in the practice that forms compassion? In general, the prayer is supposed to allow us to sink into the presence of Eternal Compassion, as Pennington's words suggest. To understand more specifically what this means, we need to look at how this practice developed and the process it teaches.

The Development of Centering Prayer

Centering Prayer was formed in the mid-1970s by Cistercian (Trappist) brothers of St. Joseph's Abbey in Spencer, Massachusetts.[21] As Father

Thomas Keating, the monastery's abbot at that time, has written, "in the wave of spiritual reawakening" sparked by the Second Vatican Council, the brothers were exposed to contemplative practices of Buddhism and Hinduism as they explored the relationship of the Roman Catholic tradition to other religious traditions.[22] In addition, the brothers noticed that the growing spiritual hunger among young people in North America was leading those seekers to eastern contemplative practices rather than to the contemplative practices of the Christian tradition in which they had been raised. Further, the brothers had come to understand that for most devout Christians, even many monks, the contemplative practices of their own tradition were reserved for a few gifted or specially situated "heroes" of the faith. In light of these concerns (and without disparaging the contemplative practices of other traditions), Father Keating posed this question to his monastic community: "Could we put the Christian tradition into a form that would be accessible to people in the active ministry today and to young people who have been instructed in an eastern technique and might be inspired to return to their Christian roots if they know there was something similar in the Christian tradition?"[23]

One of the brothers of the abbey, Father William Meninger, responded to Father Keating's question by working to develop a method of prayer he called the "Prayer of the Cloud." He based the prayer method on his understanding of an instruction in the fourteenth-century writing called *The Cloud of Unknowing*: "Lift up your heart to the Lord with a gentle stirring of love, desiring God for God's own sake, and not for God's gifts."[24] *The Cloud* describes sending a word of love in God's direction, trusting that this word would penetrate the "cloud" that lies between humans and full intimacy with God. Father Meninger refashioned *The Cloud's* one-word prayer, updating it for twentieth-century North America. Another brother of the abbey, Father Basil Pennington, began teaching the practice on retreats for groups outside the abbey. During the first retreat, in 1976, the "Prayer of the Cloud" came to be called "Centering Prayer" because of its seeming similarity with Thomas Merton's notion of "a simple way of prayer . . . centered entirely on the presence of God [so that we are] lost in God."[25]

Centering Prayer has grown in both breadth and depth since entering the common Christian lexicon. Here, however, there is but one aspect of the practice that concerns us: what Centering Prayer contributes to compassion formation. Like the prayers of the desert and Teresa's Recollection, Centering Prayer creates in us a receptacle for compassion. Centering Prayer helps us receive and become grounded in the Divine Compassion that flows constantly. Then, grounded in Compassion, we can allow that Compassion to flow through us to others.

But what exactly does Centering Prayer involve? When we practice the prayer, what is going on? The essential movements of Centering Prayer are usually stated simply, but I've found that understanding them takes explaining. So let's explore the dynamics of Centering Prayer a bit, with an eye to how these dynamics help form compassion.

The Process of Centering Prayer: Be Available to Compassion; Repeat.

Centering Prayer asks you to be available to Divine Compassion. This availability begins with *intention*. Here, I invite you to recall the foundational spiritual capacities—awareness, attention, and intention:

- *Awareness* is noticing whatever might be happening around and within you.
- *Attention* is focusing your awareness on a particular thing.
- *Intention* is wanting and willing something, even to the point of acting.

Centering Prayer downplays the spiritual capacities of awareness and attention. Let me be clear about that. It isn't that awareness and attention disappear. In fact, Centering Prayer invites you at the very least to be *aware* of whether you are available to Compassion or not. It asks you to attend occasionally and briefly to a "sacred word," as we will see. But these two spiritual capacities are not the most important ones in the practice. Instead, *intention* is the capacity that gives Centering Prayer its power.

Here's how that works. In Centering Prayer, you are asking this foundational question: "What is your intention?" The presumed answer is, "To be available to God, the eternal source of Compassion." In Centering

Prayer your intention is not simply the intention to pray, for example. Rather, it is the intention to consent to God—that is—to be totally open and available to Divine Compassion.[26]

To set the stage for this availability, Centering Prayer invites you to choose a sacred word before you enter the heart of the prayer. This word becomes "the symbol of your intention to consent to God's presence and action within."[27] The word reminds you of your *intention* to be available.

The founders of Centering Prayer were careful to define the nature of this sacred word.[28] It should be simple in form and prompt nothing in the way of emotional entanglements or conceptual musings.[29] It is like "a sign or arrow pointing in the direction you want to take."[30] Or it "is like a focusing apparatus on a camera, but the focus adjusts not an image but our intention."[31] Attention to the word and its meaning and power is not the important thing. In fact, the best sacred word is neutral; it is a reminder, a symbol of your intention. The word could even be a sound, a movement, or a mental image.[32] For instance, it could be a bell tone, an opening of your hands toward the sky, or a favorite scene in nature. Whatever the word is, its purpose is merely to return us to our intention to be available. When you say that word, hear that bell, make that motion, or imagine that image, it reinforces the thing you most want in this moment of prayer: to be available to the God of Compassion. Your intention is enough.

Says Keating, "Gently place [the word] in your awareness each time you recognize you are thinking about some other thought. . . . It only directs your intention toward God."[33] In other words, when you become aware that you are no longer open and available to God, but you are paying attention to something else (such as pondering what you'll have for lunch, feeling guilty about snapping at your daughter that morning, imagining how impressed your colleagues will be with the report you'll give next week), say the word to remind you of your intention to be available.

Centering Prayer's unique way of using sacred words sporadically, as needed, can't be overstated. For there are many other ways of using sacred words. For example, some spiritual practices repeat sacred words not on a need-to-use basis but as constant mantras. Such practices exercise awareness and attention, often to hone mental stability and concentration. These practices may value the sound of the word or use the word as a constant refrain to block out distractions, as in certain Hindu traditions.[34] Or they may invite us to focus on what the words mean. Think back, for instance, to the Desert Prayer we explored earlier. The desert sages constantly repeated, "Be pleased, O God, to deliver me. O LORD, make haste to help me!" (Ps. 70:1) The words expressed the thing they wanted God to hear, the meaning they wanted to convey: Help me, God; I need you. Similarly, the *zhikur* practices in Islam invite unbroken repetitions of the names of God.

Notice how these forms of mantra-like prayer depend mainly on attention and awareness. They focus our attention on the meaning of the words, the saying of the words, the power of the words, the trajectory of the words, and the sound of the words. And they ask us to keep our awareness tuned to where and how we focus our attention.

To illustrate Centering Prayer's unique use of sacred words, its teachers tell of a woman in a retreat with Thomas Keating. In her first attempts at Centering Prayer, the woman, a nun, had diligently followed the core Centering Prayer instruction: Whenever you notice you have turned from your intention to be available to God, say your sacred word as a reminder of that intention. But she found that she could not hold onto her intention. She kept having to say her word again and again, reminding herself over and over to be available. Discouraged, feeling herself an utter failure, she told Father Thomas that in her first twenty-minute taste of the practice she had turned away from her intention ten thousand times. "How lovely!" responded Father Thomas without missing a beat. "Ten thousand opportunities to return to God!"[35]

In Centering Prayer, such "failure" means you have countless chances to activate your intention, countless chances to exercise that vital spiritual muscle, countless chances to practice being available to God, available to receive and become grounded in Compassion. Unlike many other practices, Centering Prayer is not meant to achieve mental emptiness, stabilize concentration, strengthen awareness, or bring inner peace—though those things might happen along the way. No, it is to prepare us, open us, to be available to God. Centering Prayer is entwined with a loving hunger for God and a trust that Divine Compassion lives and acts at the core of our being. This stance defines the starting point, abiding disposition, and primary goal of the practice. Centering Prayer invites us to surrender to union with Love.

Centering Prayer assumes that God is present and active in our availability. God is active even when we don't understand, feel, or sense God's actions in any of the ways we usually understand, feel, or sense. So what is God doing? According to Father Thomas, God is always affirming "our basic goodness." God created us good and is loving us and working for our transformation no matter what we may do or think.[36]

Keating says that in Centering Prayer you will experience an ever-growing, profound yet subtle sense of being loved—a trust that all will be well despite what might seem on its surface to be great evidence to the contrary.[37] This is what it means for Centering Prayer to ground you in the Presence of Divine Compassion.

Finally, what does this grounding practice look like? Keating says that all you need to do in Centering Prayer is this:

- Choose a sacred word as the symbol of your intention to consent to God's presence and action within.
- Sitting comfortably and with eyes closed, settle briefly and silently introduce the sacred word as the symbol of your consent to God's presence and action within.
- When engaged with your thoughts, return ever so gently to the sacred word.
- At the end of the prayer period, remain in silence with eyes closed for a couple of minutes.[38]

An alternative set of guidelines, developed by Basil Pennington from a longer version he created, has only three steps: "Be with God within. Use a word to stay. Use the word to return."[39]

And if we want to get to the heart of how Centering Prayer forms compassion, we can boil the guidelines down to a spare essence:

- Be available to Divine Compassion.
- Repeat.

Centering Prayer is just that simple. It isn't about emptying your mind, moving to nothingness, stilling your thoughts, or focusing intently on something without interruption or distraction. Centering Prayer only asks us to be available to be grounded in Compassion—again and again and again.

Let's pause here and take stock of the three practices we've explored so far:

* Desert Prayer
* Teresa's Recollection
* Centering Prayer

Each in its own way offers a path for an experience of grounding in an intimate relationship with the Compassion that endlessly flows from God, the Compassionate Presence that *is* God:

* The desert sages used the constant repetition of biblical phrases to focus their attention on God's Compassion.
* Teresa used mental images of Jesus to focus attention on God's Compassion.
* Centering Prayer uses an intermittent reminder word—not for focusing our attention but to return us to our intention to be available to God's Compassionate Presence.

Whether these practices use phrases, images, or single words, or whether they engage our attention, awareness, or intention, they still invite us into a stance of being grounded in Compassion. In every case, the "Compassion Capacity" of intimacy is at work. In other words, there is not a single, correct way to become grounded in Compassion. Instead, the traditions have developed a variety of paths to meet the needs of the many, varied people who long to be formed in the compassionate image of God. The three practices we have explored so far only offer a hint of the many possibilities available.

I hope you will take this hint of variety as an invitation to look for the practice that most fully grounds your own life in Divine Compassion.

That practice will provide the starting place and the secure, abiding touchpoint for cultivating compassion in your life and in the world.

Review and Practice

In this chapter, we explored three practices that help us ground ourselves in the Divine Compassion that constantly flows to, within, and through all things: Desert Prayer, Recollection, and Centering Prayer. Each one offers its own path, highlighting spiritual longings, needs, sensibilities, styles, and spiritual capacities.

- In Desert Prayer, the ancient sages gave themselves over to the security and care of God. Their practice emphasized these spiritual capacities:

  - Foundational Capacity: **Attention**. They focused their attention on repeating biblical phrases—a commitment to "pray without ceasing."

  - Compassion Capacity: **Intimacy**. Through repetition of the biblical phrases they turned themselves fully to God, seeking a deep and lasting sense of safe, secure communion with God, a grounding in Divine Compassion.

- In Recollection, Teresa of Avila invites us to envision our interior lives as a crowd of people being gathered into the presence of a King, God. In this way, her practice highlighted these spiritual capacities:

  - Foundational Capacity: **Attention**. She focused laser-like on what was going on with the crowd of feelings, images, physical sensations, and thoughts within her.

  - Compassion Capacities: **Imagination** and **Intimacy**. She used her imagination to turn her inner experiences into a dynamic story. The story carried her into a sense of being intimately grounded in a living Divine Presence.

- Centering Prayer invites us to open ourselves again and again to be available to the Presence of Compassion. It highlights these spiritual capacities:

▲ Foundational Capacity: **Intention**. In Centering Prayer, we have a simple purpose, a singular intention to keep opening to Divine Compassion. We use a sacred word to remind us to do that.

▲ Compassion Capacity: **Intimacy**. Centering Prayer does not move toward a place of emptiness. Rather, it helps the soul respond to its innate desire to experience the deep warmth of being filled by and grounded in Divine Presence.

In addition to these practices, many others may help us become grounded in Divine Compassion. Below are a few examples with which you may wish to experiment. These are based on exercises within the Compassion Practice, which we will explore more fully in chapter 5. It may help to set a timer, perhaps with a gentle chime, before you begin such processes so you don't have to worry about when you should end. I recommend a twenty-minute period, but if you are not used to such practices, you may wish to start out with just a few minutes at a time and gradually work up to twenty.

Breathing Divine Compassion

There are many ways to ground yourself in the Presence of Compassion using your breath. The following is a simple form:

* Settle yourself into a comfortable position that allows for alertness.
* Gently draw your attention to your breathing, the rise and fall of your abdomen.
* Do not modify your breathing, but notice its natural flow. Follow it in and out with your attention.
* Begin to count your breaths . . . up to ten.
* Rest for a time with your breathing, noticing it or not, experiencing the calm in your body.

* At some point, with each in-breath, silently note to yourself, *I breathe in Divine Compassion.* And with each out-breath, silently note, *I breathe with Divine Compassion.*
* As the exercise ends, offer an expression of gratitude for this time.

Meditating on a Sacred Moment[40]

This exercise engages your memory to let the specific moments of your life ground you in the Presence of Divine Compassion.

* Take several deep, gentle breaths, allowing yourself to settle into stillness.
* Become aware of various moments in your week or life where you sense that the Sacred was present—moments of life, love, joy, wonder, or heightened immediacy. These may be intense and unforgettable moments or simple and mundane whispers of Presence. Of the various moments that come to you, allow one to emerge as the focus for the rest of this prayer exercise.
* Remember this moment by returning to it in your imagination.
    ▲ Recall what was going on in your life at the time, where you were, and whom you were with.
    ▲ Reexperience the sensory details of the moment—the sights, sounds, smells, tastes, and bodily sensations.
    ▲ Remember how the Sacred became present and what this Presence felt like.
* Allow the Presence of the Sacred to expand once more within you, filling you and surrounding you; for as long as it feels right, rest in and savor this Presence. As you continue to rest in this Presence, allow a symbol to come to you that embodies the essence of this Presence—a healing light perhaps, a divine figure, or a warm embrace. Allow this symbol of Sacred Presence to fill your awareness so that you can access it and return to it when you feel the need.

- In preparing to conclude this practice, discern if there is an invitation from the Sacred for how you might allow the grace of this prayer to extend into your daily life.

Compassion Along the Way

Many spiritual practices and exercises invite you to set aside time in your schedule to engage them, as the two above do. But you may find that you need to be grounded in a sense of Divine Compassion during difficult situations or encounters throughout the day. The exercises below address this moment-to-moment need by drawing on the grounding that is formed in "Meditating on a Sacred Moment" and "Breathing Divine Compassion." Practiced in the heat of the moment, in combination or alone, they can help you return to grounding in Compassion any time you notice yourself reacting in a way that leads to a 3F state.

BREATHING IN COMPASSION

- Throughout your day, whenever you notice a shift toward reactivity, a sense of being ungrounded, turn your attention to your breathing. This can happen subtly, without others even knowing you are doing it.
- Gently allow your breath to flow deeply into your abdomen and gently exhale fully.
- This attentive breathing may be enough, but you may wish to match your breath to thoughts:
  - ▲ With each in-breath, wordlessly repeat, *Divine Compassion...*
  - ▲ With each out-breath, wordlessly repeat, *... breathes in me.*

SACRED PRESENCE IN THIS MOMENT

- Throughout your day, whenever you notice a shift toward reactivity, a sense of being ungrounded, turn your memory to the Symbol of Sacred Presence that came to you in your experience of "Meditating on a Sacred Moment." This can happen subtly in the "background" of your attention, even as you go about whatever task is at hand.

- Allow this symbol to activate your imagination, returning you to the experience of Sacred Presence it has evoked for you. For instance, if your Symbol of Sacred Presence was an image of you sitting in a beautiful garden in warm sunlight, enter into the feelings of that symbol as much as possible in the moment. Often, just the slightest reminder of it will be enough.

CHAPTER 3

Compassion Practices for Yourself

A few years ago, I helped facilitate a multiday retreat that taught contemplative practices for leadership development. During the initial introductions, one of the participants, a thirty-something, kind, gentle lay leader named Margaret, told me she was there because she wanted to help her congregation strengthen its education and outreach efforts.

It soon became clear that strengthening her leadership skills was going to be a stretch for Margaret. She was withdrawn, unsure of herself, and shy about speaking her wisdom. In the small-group training sessions, she consistently refused to take her turn in the skill-development role-plays. In private, Margaret confided that she was overwhelmed and terrified—both in the retreat and in her life. The only aspects of the retreat she could handle, she said, were the daily contemplative-prayer times of silence, scripture, and sung chants.

Recognizing Margaret's struggles, everyone encouraged her to pay attention to what she needed and to participate as she could. And that is what Margaret did. Each day she showed up, joined the small-group sessions and plenaries, and participated in the communal contemplative-prayer times. As far as anyone could tell, Margaret remained the pleasant, leadership-challenged person she had been when she had arrived on the first day of the retreat.

But in the last hour of the retreat something amazing happened. As we were debriefing and saying our goodbyes, a new Margaret appeared, strong, self-assured, and hopeful. When her turn to speak came, instead of offering a timid platitude, she quietly and confidently shared what had happened with her in the past days. Margaret began by outlining the defining trauma of her childhood. Her mother had gone into labor with her while being physically abused by Margaret's father. Her father named her after his mother, whom he hated because she had abused him her whole life—a fact that Margaret's parents told her as soon as she could talk—and never let her forget.

Margaret spent over three decades feeling nothing but shame and hopelessness in the face of this childhood trauma. It stifled her creativity, her desire to serve others, her dreams of leadership in the church. But being in this retreat, she said, changed all of that. For the first time in her life, Margaret had a true sense of grounding in Divine Compassion, an experience of God's love for her. As that sense deepened and expanded, she began to see herself from the perspective of God's loving compassion. What she saw was a gifted, committed woman who longed to help others and yearned to release her creative energies for leadership in her community. To mark this opening, Margaret had decided to change her name. No longer would she go by the name of a woman everyone despised. Now she would be Grace, her middle name, and the name of an aunt who had been Grace's sole refuge and source of love in her childhood.

I admit that at the time I was skeptical when I heard Margaret's story. I had a hard time believing that such a transformation could have taken place in such a short time. But my skepticism didn't last; Margaret was as good as her word. The next time I saw her, about a year after that contemplative leadership retreat, she had legally changed her first name to Grace. I learned that she had entered intensive spiritual direction and psychological therapy, both acts of self-compassion. And she had clearly identified her gifts and honed them. Instead of remaining a church-leader-wannabe, she had become a dynamic force for change in her congregation as well as in her regional-church structure. She was now being called upon to design leadership-training curricula and to guide others in teaching it; she had been asked to chair a regional education and outreach effort; and she was considering entering seminary.

Even Grace's personal presence showed change. Where Margaret had been hesitant, Grace was forthright; where Margaret had been self-denigrating, Grace was self-confident; where Margaret had described her ineptitude, Grace showed skillful creativity. The kindness, care, and commitment remained. But shame-filled hopelessness had been replaced by wise, restorative compassion in action—compassion offered not only to the world but also to herself.

Margaret's story shows us how genuine compassion unfolds: It begins with the experience of grounding in the Presence of Compassion and moves to an experience of offering compassion to yourself. Only then can true compassion for others fully emerge. Through the retreat time, Margaret received Divine Compassion: She asked Compassion to keep her secure, as the Desert Prayer would put it; or Recollected herself within Compassion, as Teresa of Avila would describe it; or made herself available to Compassion, in the words of Centering Prayer.

This foundation of grounding in Compassion allowed Margaret to offer compassion to herself. After grounding in the Presence of Compassion, she could recognize what she needed and give herself a gift—a new name, the symbol of her true self. This gift sealed the transformation. It gave Margaret an abiding symbol of the compassion she received and the compassion she had offered herself. Margaret had felt a core commitment to faithful service that nudged her to the retreat. There, she found a way to become grounded in the Divine Compassion she sought in her life. But only by then turning to offer compassion to herself could she become the compassionate person she longed to be.

The Jesus Prayer

The pattern of self-compassion that Margaret discovered appeared in early Christianity in a practice that came to be known as the Jesus Prayer. By the fifth century, North-African and Middle-Eastern Christians had begun reciting its simple words to help them turn compassion toward themselves. The Jesus Prayer, though not often named as a compassion practice, can cultivate self-compassion.

The Jesus Prayer appears to be straightforward. At the most basic level you merely repeat the words "Lord Jesus Christ, son of God, have compassion on me."[1] The words can appear to be little more than a request for Divine Compassion. The prayer is a practice for *receiving* compassion rather than for *self*-compassion. But what the words say merely scratches the surface of the power of this compassion practice. We experience the power of the prayer when it moves us from a place of receiving Divine Compassion to a place where we offer compassion to ourselves.

The Jesus Prayer assumes human beings have three dimensions: body, mind, and heart. These three dimensions of the person intertwine; whatever happens with one affects the other two. The body is our physical dimension. It brings us knowledge through the senses. The mind is the aspect that makes us "something alive, as opposed to an inanimate mass of flesh." It brings us knowledge through our intellect. The heart is the dimension that allows us "to enter into communion with God" in spiritual maturity or God-likeness (divinization). We can think of heart as the dimension that connects and integrates all aspects of our humanness. It brings us knowledge in a special way, "through a mystical perception that transcends . . . ordinary rational processes."[2]

The Jesus Prayer has three degrees that correspond with the three dimensions of humanness: prayer of the body, prayer of the mind, and prayer of the heart.[3]

The first dimension, *prayer of the body*, consists of reading or reciting the words of the Jesus Prayer while standing, kneeling, or making prostrations: "Jesus Christ, Son of God, have compassion on me." You may mouth the words or speak them aloud. Some teachers even describe how the repetition of the words of the prayer may be matched with the rhythms of breathing. Teachers stress that the words and the repetition of the words are not magical. Instead, the power of the prayer comes from the One to whom it is directed: Christ.[4] And transformation comes through the prayer's cultivation of an ever-more-intimate relationship with God through Christ.

For this reason, the prayer invites you to concentrate not only on speaking the words but on the meaning of what is being said, repeating the words slowly and carefully to focus on their significance. As one teaching puts it, you are to keep "listening to the words of the prayer, learning from them and pondering over them."[5] Another teaching says that as you repeat the words, they begin to evoke "a vivid awareness of the immediate all-embracing experience" of Christ that includes "a sense of yearning and tender love."[6] This prayer of the body begins to turn your entire being to recall God and to experience the Presence of God—a stance the tradition calls *mindfulness*.[7]

The second dimension, *prayer of the mind*, intensifies the mindfulness that began in the prayer of the body. As mental concentration takes over and intensifies, speaking the words becomes less important, and the mind prays without the body mouthing the words at all. This prayer of the mind requires less human effort than the prayer of the body. In fact, the mind may not even be repeating the words. Instead, "the Prayer gradually acquires a rhythm of its own, at times singing within us almost spontaneously, without any conscious act of will on our part [as if] we have within us 'a small murmuring stream.'"[8] This growing sense of the prayer continuing without effort brings the practice to the third level.

The third dimension, *prayer of the heart*, is often called "the mind in the heart" because the entire being is now involved in prayer. When the mind enters the heart, you pray "not only with words [formed by the body] but with the mind, and not only with the mind but with the heart, so that the mind understands and sees clearly what is said in words, and the heart feels what the mind is thinking."[9] How do you know that the mind is in the heart? You know it because at that point the prayer is unceasing, effortless. You are no longer praying the prayer; the prayer is praying you. The prayer fills you with a deep experience of feeling God's compassionate presence. You experience a profound intimacy with God, rather than simply knowing about God. Gregory of Sinai called this a "warmth produced in the heart."[10] This heartfelt "sense of spiritual warmth—the 'burning of the spirit' within us" marks the Jesus Prayer as a practice for receiving Divine Compassion.[11]

So, yes, the Jesus Prayer is a practice of grounding in God's compassion. But here's the bigger point: The Jesus Prayer will move you beyond this deep sense of grounding in Compassion; it will give you a way to offer yourself compassion. It is a self-compassion practice.

Even the simple move to pray the Jesus Prayer was an act of self-compassion for the ancient people of faith who developed it. The religion of their day tended to tell them that they were full of sin, missing the mark in every moment, unworthy of God's attention. Still, even in the face of this burdensome message, they were bold enough to approach God and ask for the compassion they believed lay at the heart of the good news.

The very act of praying the prayer has been an act of self-compassion for many Christians over the ages.

Permission to boldly seek compassion is not the only way in which the Jesus Prayer offers a path to self-compassion. When "the prayer begins to pray us"—that is, when the mind enters the heart—we begin to take on the attitudes of Christ; we begin to share Christ's ability to love. The spiritual warmth that comes in the prayer is the "'flame of grace' kindled in the heart."[12] It is Compassion living within us. The Jesus Prayer leads us to become more and more like Jesus, "gazing favorably on everything, and considering it from God's point of view."[13] And "everything" includes our selves. The prayer brings us to a place where it heals us, restores us, and frees us enough to offer compassion even to ourselves. We become so filled with Divine Compassion that when we turn to look at our own lives, we see ourselves from Jesus' perspective, and we act toward ourselves with the compassion of Jesus.

The Jesus Prayer is my go-to prayer during my day. I constantly need compassion from God and from myself. I pray "Have compassion on me" again and again, praying without ceasing, entering the Divine Compassion that is directed toward me, becoming the image of that Compassion, becoming compassion itself—even to the point of becoming compassionate toward myself. I can understand and forgive myself as I would a family member I love who lives in fear, regret, or guilt.

This is what happened to my friend Grace as she changed her name from Margaret. She traveled the path carved out by the Jesus Prayer. During her leadership-formation retreat, she prayed unceasingly. Divine Compassion warmed her heart until she could be compassionate to herself, even to the point of giving herself a new name to launch her new life. From that place of self-compassion, she was freed to compassionately serve others.

Having seen how self-compassion transformed Grace's life and the lives of so many others, I can't help wondering again at the fact that Christianity has largely skipped over Jesus' invitation to love ourselves. Wise, strong, effective, appropriate compassion for others can only grow from a place of self-compassion. How ironic that this ancient Christian prayer—the oldest one still in use outside of scripture—is, in fact, a practice of self-compassion.

Review and Practice

Here are some key points of review for deepening understanding and practice of the Jesus Prayer:

- The Jesus Prayer, the oldest Christian prayer formula still in wide use, is a mantra-like meditative practice with roots in the fifth century.
- The prayer invites us to attend to the meaning of its words as we repeat them. The meanings of the words help us focus on God, remember God, be mindful of God, and strengthen our intimate experience of loving relationship with God. This attention to the meaning and focus of the words contrasts with other practices that use vocal repetition. For instance, Centering Prayer asks us to choose a sacred word that is meaning-neutral, and it is a reminder to return to our intention to be available to God.
- The movements of the Jesus Prayer correspond with dimensions of humanness: prayer of the body moves to prayer of the mind, which becomes holistic prayer of the heart.
- The repetition of the words of the prayer leads to an interior freedom and stability filled with deep emotions, including intimacy with God and an experience of sharing in the compassion of Jesus. This differs from other mantric traditions in which repetition is meant to lead to a release from emotions, as well as a quelling of the words and thoughts connected to them.
- The prayer involves a settling in to an experience of receiving complete compassion for ourselves—particularly a forgiving freedom from the binding power of guilt and shame that is tied to a dominating sense of unworthiness. The prayer moves us to an experience of seeing ourselves from God's compassionate perspective—which leads us to compassion for ourselves.
- The Jesus Prayer stands in a line of Christian contemplative practices that take a clearing approach to the difficult interior stuff that comes up. That is, when so-called passions appear, the processes of the Jesus Prayer tend toward trying to clear them away, either by human effort or by overwhelming them

with God's good presence. This approach assumes that certain impulses are by their nature bad, a sort of infection to eradicate. Other practices (for example, those that rise out of the Ignatian tradition informed by the anthropology described by Thomas Aquinas) take a transforming approach. They assume that the original impulse was created good and simply needs to be healed, realigned, or brought into harmony.[14] So the practice works with the passion, rather than trying to clear it away.

- The Jesus Prayer strongly engages two of the three Foundational Capacities: intention and attention. The third, awareness, plays a smaller role. We need strong *intention* to keep repeating the words of the prayer in the "prayer of the body" phase of the practice. And we need a great deal of *attention* to stay focused on the meanings of the words and on the Divine Presence they point to.

- In the Jesus Prayer, the basic capacities of attention and intention, however necessary, serve primarily as tools for building a path to two of the Compassion Capacities: *intimacy* and *feelings*. This prayer is primarily about intimacy with Divine Presence. It invites us to offer ourselves fully to God, trusting that as we pray the prayer, a sense of intimacy with the Presence of Divine Compassion will grow in us. What's more, that sense of intimacy will contain feelings, the emotions of warm connections with God that form compassion for ourselves and for the entire universe.

- Notice that the third compassion capacity, *imagination*, does not come into play in the Jesus Prayer. In fact, traditionally teachers have seen imagination as stifling intimacy with the Divine Presence. Some have even seen it as dangerous, capturing our attention in fantasies that carry us away from Godward mindfulness.[15] Instead, these teachers invite us to focus our entire beings on the prayer's words, their meanings, and especially their subject. This leaves no opportunity for diversionary fantasies; the words, their meanings, growing intimacy with Divine Compassion, and deepening feelings of warmth and compassion expand to fill all the spaces in our beings.

The Prayer of Your Heart

In practicing the Jesus Prayer, you may wish to use the traditional form, or you may prefer to explore more contemporary options, versions that retain an invitation to Divinely-grounded self-compassion but in language that more closely matches your own spiritual sensibilities. If that is true for you, it may be helpful to recall that the Jesus Prayer has been the primary practice in the "Prayer of the Heart" tradition. Those who practice it find that its words give expression to the heart's longing for all-encompassing Compassion, the ultimate yearning of a person's entire being. What words would express that longing for you? The "Prayer of Your Heart" is composed of *your* words.

Here are some examples to inspire you to form the unique practice that is the "Prayer of Your Heart":

* "Be with me, Jesus [on the in-breath], full of Compassion [on the out-breath]."
* "Compassion, fill me [on the in-breath]; Compassion for me [on the out-breath]."
* "Compassion to me [on the in-breath]; Compassion through me [on the out-breath]."

I invite you to experiment with words for the prayer that match the longing of your own heart for Compassion, even for self-compassion. Let those words draw you to a deep sense of compassion for yourself through a grounding in Divine Compassion.

CHAPTER 4

Compassion Practices for Others

A few years ago, my friend Frank Rogers drove to the southern California mountain park where he runs each morning. Frank is a professor of spiritual formation, a novelist, a retreat leader and spiritual director, a sought-after teacher of compassion, and the loving father of Justin. On this morning, Frank's primary role (as usual) was father. Justin's beloved Siberian husky, Misty, had recently died of cancer. Frank had promised that on this morning he would memorialize Justin's twelve-year relationship with Misty by scattering some of Misty's ashes on the trails she had roamed. But there was a glitch: Frank had very little time before his first appointment of the day, and he could find no place to park his car. The lots were full; the street spots were taken; Frank's window of opportunity was closing.

Frank began circling the neighborhoods near the running trails, searching, hoping, longing for a place to legally leave his car. He was determined to complete his labor of parental love. Finally, as he was about to give up, Frank found one empty spot. It was on a residential street that allowed public parking near the trails where Misty had loved to run. This was, thought Frank, a small blessing of the task at hand. He parked, grabbed all he needed for the memorial trail run, and jumped out of the car. But before he could start jogging away, he saw a terrifying sight.

Frank describes what happened:

A large man was barreling down the driveway toward me, a steel rake in hand, outstretched and menacing. "What're you doing?! You're parking right in front of my house!"

Being the man of compassion that I am, I instinctively yelled back, "What? I'm not doing anything wrong!" I pointed to the public parking sign. "It says so right there."

"You're right in front of my house!" he yelled louder, jabbing with his rake. "My bushes! My lawn! My property!"

"But I'm on the street!" I yelled back. "I'm not touching your property! Really! It's totally legal to park here!"

The man scowled. He seemed ready to spit, to swear, to take a swing. Instead he blasted me with, "You're not going to help me, are you? You're not going to help me! Fine! The hell with all of you!"[1]

Frank was frozen in place, tense, confused. He wondered if he should defend himself, or get in his car and take off, or stand his ground in silence. Frank had entered a 3F state, the fight-flight-freeze reaction. But before Frank's reactions had a chance to grow, the man turned and stormed back toward the house.

At this point, Frank saw two paths before him. The first was the path of animosity, some version of the automatic 3F state Frank felt in the heat of the protective yelling and posturing. The second path was the way of compassion.

For decades Frank had been focused on following the Divine invitation to compassion. He had been engaging in daily compassion-forming practices for most of those years. It now occurred to him that this situation was exactly the kind of challenge those practices were preparing him for.

Even Frank, a revered teacher of compassion, admits to feeling conflicted: The parts of him that were caught up in the 3F state wanted to protect his life by fighting, freezing, or fleeing. At the same time, another part of him wanted to find a way that was true to his commitment to compassion for all people, even those his body instinctively perceived as enemies.

What did Frank do when he noticed these conflicted inclinations? Here, in Frank's words, is what happened:

I gathered my courage, walked up to the man's door, and rang the bell. He answered, surprised that I was there, and on guard for what I might want.

"Sir," I said. "I am really sorry. I just reacted a few minutes ago and I did not hear what you were saying. I can see that it really bothers you to have cars parked so close to your yard. People can be careless; I'm sure it's frustrating. I'm happy to move mine. I just wanted you to know that I get it; and I'm sorry for not hearing it before."

He eyed me, still skeptical.

"People park here all the time," he reinforced. "They don't care—it's somebody's home. People live here."

"I know," I said. "I'm sorry I didn't realize it before. I was just in a hurry. My dog died, my son's dog, really. She loved that trail. I just wanted to scatter some of her ashes, then get back to my boy."

He eyed me some more, something softening. "Your dog," he said, "your boy's dog—she died, huh?" I nodded. "Yeah. My girl had a dog too. It was killed in the fighting." He looked off as if returning to some land far away. Then he continued, softer still. "You know why I hate the people parking their cars in front of my house?" I didn't. He let out a sigh. "We're from Iraq. Baghdad." He shook his head. "Sometimes the people, they parked their cars in front of our apartment. One day, one of them explodes. Right in front of our house. Not twenty minutes before, my girl, my six-year-old, is playing on that street. We come to America. Now she can't sleep. Each morning, she looks out, cars parked in front of our house even here. She begs me, but what can I do? Tell me, what is a father to do?"

I looked at him. His aggression had dissipated. My defensiveness had too. I had no answers. A child's terror silences all. Still, somehow, we both knew. The parking of my car no longer mattered. All that did was the meeting on that porch. Two dads, bearing the sorrow of their children, seeking refuge in a world of violence and loss.[2]

Frank's courageous compassion sparked the same in his (former) enemy. I imagine you have also found this to be true in your own life. And Christian sages over the centuries have known the same. They developed spiritual practices that explicitly help us hone our ability to offer compassion to others, even those we find to be difficult, unlovable, or antagonistic.

We'll explore three examples of practices that form compassion for others. Two come from a medieval collection of writings called *Meditations on the Life of Christ*; they form compassion both for people who are dear to us and for people we might experience as enemies. The third practice comes from the sixteenth-century "Spiritual Exercises of Ignatius of Loyola." It expands compassion into an abiding, general stance toward all people and all creation.

Meditations on the Life of Christ

In medieval Europe, many writings appeared that contained spiritual practices derived from the life of Jesus. The most influential was the thirteenth-century Latin writing called *Meditations on the Life of Christ*.[3] Because of its popularity, many have used its title as a generic term for the multitude of similar medieval writings.

Like the other practices we've considered, the practices in the many versions of the *Meditations* are not called compassion practices. But a number describe how to form compassion for others through using the power of imagination. In fact, the more imagination the better.[4] The teachers of the *Meditations* tradition had learned that, for many people, imagination could intensify beneficial emotions, thoughts, and behaviors in a way that enhanced the spiritual life.

The *Meditations* contain detailed, graphic accounts of key moments in the life, death, and resurrection of Jesus. The medieval version of today's virtual reality games, *Meditations* immersed people in an experience of being there even when they weren't. Teachers often read the texts aloud to individuals or groups, much like theatrical scripts, which surely added possibilities for drawing people into an experience of virtual reality, complete with audience participation.[5] Lacking virtual-reality goggles, the teachers asked students to imagine themselves in a scene with Jesus: "Imagine yourself in that place at that time. What do you see, taste, hear, feel, smell, touch?" And sometimes the text asks for problems to be solved or poses questions on the order of "What would you have done if you had been there?" The authors of the writings followed the common belief that there are "spiritual senses" that parallel our physical senses.[6] If we exercise those spiritual senses, our entire beings will be transformed from the inside out.

The practices in the *Meditations* build compassion for two groups of "others," both those people who are dear to us and those whom we might experience as enemies in some respect. For each of these two groups of people, *Meditations* provides a compassion practice. We'll look at these one at a time, beginning (as the *Meditations* do) with the group of people who are dear to us—our loved ones, our friends, or those we admire. Then we'll look at the *Meditations'* process for forming compassion for the people we find more difficult, those we experience as threatening or harmful—those we might refer to as enemies.

Compassion for Those Dear to Us

To build compassion for those dear to us, the *Meditations* first guides us to consider Jesus, especially his suffering on the cross. The narrator of the story asks us to imagine the scene described in one of the crucifixion accounts, to ponder questions about the situation and our feelings, to behold in our imaginations the suffering Jesus, to see him, to hear his words, to embrace him. We aren't to observe the scene from a distance; we are to imagine ourselves as actors in the drama. Such vivid imaginings will evoke profound compassion.

To help us build compassion for those dear to us, the *Meditations* begins by focusing our attention on Jesus. The narrator believes Jesus is so dear to us that we will naturally feel compassion for him when we imagine him suffering:

> Whoever . . . would busy himself with all his heart and all his mind and meditate on [Jesus' crucifixion] and all its circum-stances would be changed and brought into . . . new compas-sion. . . . To achieve this state . . . a man . . . must make himself present . . . as if he saw with his bodily eye all the things that

happened around the cross regarding the glorious Passion of our Lord Jesus. . . . How much compassion is [then] stirred. . . ?[7]

Now, with inward compassion, behold him here . . . , passing fair and young a man, most innocent and most lovely, in that manner all rent and wounded, and all bloody and naked . . . forsaken by God and without all manner of succor or help.[8]

Then also, if thou behold well thy Lord, thou might have here matter enough of high compassion, seeing him so tormented. . . .[9]

The narrator trusts that Jesus is not the only person in the story who is dear to us. We can exercise our compassion muscle a bit more by imagining the pain of Jesus' mother and others who love him.[10] First comes Mary, Jesus' mother: "[W]hat state at that time was his mother's soul in when she saw him so painfully fail, weep and die? Verily, I believe that from the multitude of her anguishes she was all out of herself . . . like one half dead[11] . . . ." For our lady hangs on the cross with her dear son in spirit. . . ."[12] Then the narrator directs our attention to Mary Magdalene, John, and "two sisters of our lady . . . all full of sorrow and bitterness, and therefore they wept sore without remedy. . . ."[13]

From the perspective of our own time, such emotionally charged, dramatic presentations may seem over the top, perhaps even manipulative. On the other hand, they are probably no more than we are used to experiencing from movies, especially 3-D and Imax versions, that evoke and intensify our emotions by flooding us with vivid images. And they are no more than we experience in advertisements for certain charities, in which pictures of suffering children move us to join in efforts to help them.

We have an instinct for compassion. Images of suffering activate that instinct. Using images, perceived with the eyes or in the imagination, to trigger emotions for a compassionate response is a timeless practice. Used appropriately, wisely, and with right intention, the imagination can expand compassionate action in the world in ways that heal and free.

Compassion for Enemies

The examples we've looked at so far use imagination to grow compassion for those dear to us. But the *Meditations* also describes a way to grow compassion for those we find difficult, those we experience in some way as antagonists or even enemies. Ultimately, this is our greatest challenge, and it is one we cannot ignore. Jesus, after all, invites us to follow this most difficult of paths.

I want to be clear that when I use the term "enemy" I'm not necessarily talking about a person who's out to harm me or someone I care about. When I talk about enemies here, I'm referring to how we experience people, whether there is actual antagonism involved or not. Sometimes people do put us or those we care for in danger in some way. Often, though, I find myself feeling hostile toward someone or feeling threatened by this person, even as I notice that people I trust and care for have perfectly wonderful relationships with this person.

Psychologists could name many reasons for such feelings of hostility. Suppose, for instance, I have an immediate, automatic, negative reaction to a new acquaintance, someone who strikes everyone else as kind and generous. I don't even know the man; my reaction has nothing to do with who he is. Instead, maybe his voice reminds me of someone who harmed me in my childhood, so I transfer my fear onto him. Or maybe the way he dresses reminds me of something I so dislike about myself that I project that dislike onto him. Upon reflection, I'm not actually experiencing *him*. I am only experiencing my own fears or insecurities through my encounter with him. He *feels* like an enemy to me. In Frank's parking-place story, Frank's presence in a parked car triggered this reaction in the man who confronted him. Frank simply needed a place to put his car.

The man's whole being screamed, "Enemy!"

Normally we use the term *enemy* to refer to someone who would harm us if given the chance. But I want to broaden it to include all those people we find to be difficult in big and small ways, real and imagined, consciously or unconsciously, truly threatening or not. I am using the term *enemy* to refer to how I experience certain people, regardless of whether they wish me harm or not. Such people are the "difficult others" in my life. They appear all the time, or at least they do for me. I imagine that to be true for you too. It's vital for me to be able to offer compassion to these difficult others whether they endanger me or not.

What kind of practice builds compassion toward difficult people, people we experience as enemies? According to the *Meditations,* cultivating compassion for enemies looks a lot like the practice for cultivating compassion toward those dear to us: It asks us to imagine ourselves into a scene that evokes compassion in us.

But the compassion-for-enemies practice takes us a step further. As Dan Merkur notes, it asks us to enter into *Jesus' own experience* of compassion.[14] It invites us "to stir . . . to melting in" Jesus as he suffers— that is, to imaginatively meld our emotions with Christ's emotions as he hangs on the cross.[15] But we aren't to focus on his feelings of pain. Instead, we are to enter his feelings of love. Here's how the *Meditations* puts it:

> We shall consider Christ's passion with advisement and with great soberness and strive for to feel through touching of his grace, relenting of our hearts by a perfect transforming into his blessed love.[16]
>
> [In this way one will be] wholly converted into . . . Jesus Christ crucified.[17]

I know of no other spiritual-practice tradition that guides us so fully into Jesus' inner experiences. Imagining ourselves as Jesus is normally off limits in the Christian tradition, perhaps to keep Messiah complexes at bay. But maybe the writers of the *Meditations* found that loving enemies is so difficult and important that to cultivate it we need to explore territory that is normally off limits; we need to unite with Christ by sharing Jesus' own emotions.

For those wise teachers, only by imaginatively entering Christ's experience on the cross, uniting our emotions with those of Jesus, can we become compassionate in the way that Christ was. We will then act to ease the suffering of others through the deeds of compassion that Jesus taught and modeled.[18] The culmination and greatest of these deeds is to forgive those we experience as enemies:

> All these deeds of compassion showed our Lord on the cross, and a token of greatest pity also, when he prayed his Father for them that slew him and said thus: "Father forgive them. . . ." Right so shall we do [to] forgive them that trespass against us . . . that our soul might be in peace with them, and they with us. . . .[19]

Genuinely compassionate action for enemies, even those who harm us, grows as we imagine ourselves sharing in Jesus's experience of offering compassion even as he suffered. We experience what Jesus experiences. The Christian spiritual traditions describe this as becoming the image of Christ or entering into union with God. Although many people have thought of "union with God" as disengaging from life in the world, Christian compassion practices show the opposite: The deeper the union with God, the more deeply we engage life in the world, offering compassion even to those we experience as enemies. Through that compassion, enemies become reconciled, "in peace" with one another.

The *Meditations* arose in a time and place that saw Christians demonizing the Jewish community by describing Jews as the enemies who killed Jesus. Historians point out that these texts were a product of their time; they carry anti-Semitic undertones. To ignore their latent anti-Semitism is to ignore Jesus' invitation to genuine compassion. Acknowledging this and other forms of vilification, however hidden they may be, contributes to their elimination.

Thankfully the *Meditations'* own compassion practices can help in the effort to eliminate demonizing behavior and to expand genuine, restorative compassion in the world. The specifics of the practices themselves ultimately do not focus on identifying or blaming those who crucified Jesus. Rather, they assert that it is right to offer compassion as Jesus did, as God does—even to those we may be tempted to vilify. In the midst of all movements to the contrary, true compassion can shine through.

Ignatian Contemplation to Attain Love

The *Meditations* has shown us compassion practices for those who are dear to us and for those who seem difficult to us. But Christian compassion practices don't stop there. Some intentionally move us to a *stance* of compassion—an abiding attitude of active compassion toward all people, all things, all creation. Scientists call this a *trait*—that is, an ingrained characteristic—as opposed to a *state*, which is temporary. The traditional practice that names this process of developing the trait of engaged compassion more clearly than others comes from the writings of Ignatius of Loyola, a sixteenth-century Spanish mystic-reformer.

Ignatius's compassion practice is the "Contemplation to Attain Love." Before we look at the practice itself, it can be helpful to get a sense of what role it played in Ignatius's teachings on the spiritual life.

Ignatius founded the Jesuits—a religious order of "contemplatives in action"—to live out compassion in the world rather than in monasteries. For Ignatius, the path toward union with God was a world-engaged process. This was not the norm in his day (or in ours, for that matter).

Unlike Ignatius, some other Christian spiritual traditions describe the spiritual path as ascending to holiness, using a metaphor of climbing a ladder to heaven. This way assumes that the world is full of distractions and blocks that keep us from God. In this view, we must ignore the distractions and clear away the blocks so that we can follow the path that climbs from the world up to heaven.

Ignatius flips that metaphor around. He points us toward a spiritual path that follows Christ *into* the world, not away from it. The Ignatian tradition teaches that each "distraction" or "block" is a blessing. Why? Because it is a new opportunity for discerning how to follow the path more closely, more freely. Everything life brings us—each challenge, pain, joy, delight, whether within us or around us—is an invitation to discernment. Each one is a chance to refine our sense of our vocation, to understand who we are within Divine Grace, to heal and free us, to clarify our unique way of helping heal and free others. Ignatius assumed we all have unique gifts, skills, and sensibilities. The unique package of humanness that we bring to our service in the world is our image of Christ in the world. Our unique lives shape what "union with God" looks like, a you-shaped image of God.

To help you form the you-shaped image of God in the world, Ignatius designed a month-long intensive series of what he called "spiritual exercises."[20] The heart of these exercises involves imagining yourself living Jesus' life along with him, talking with him, sharing his experiences, noticing how you feel, what you think, and what you do as you follow his path in life. These exercises follow in the tradition of the practices in the *Meditations on the Life of Christ*, with their focus on imagining scenes, feelings, and thoughts. Following the model of the *Meditations*, "The Spiritual Exercises of Ignatius of Loyola" invites you into Gospel scenes of Jesus healing and teaching, asks you to imagine yourself at the foot of the cross, and encourages you to envision encountering the risen Christ. The "Spiritual Exercises" places you in the scenes described by the Gospels and asks repeatedly some version of "What do you see? Feel? Hear? Touch? Say? Think?" That is how you infuse your experience, your life, with the way of Jesus—with active, loving compassion in the unique form your life gives it. Your feelings and imagination are powerful tools for your deep, expansive transformation. In fact, the transformative power of this ancient imaginative process has been affirmed in the approaches of modern psychology. For instance, the renowned psychologist Carl Jung used Ignatius's "Spiritual Exercises" as a resource in developing "active imagination" for his therapeutic work.[21]

Ignatius's "Spiritual Exercises" gradually build a life of compassion, engaging our emotions and imagination to unite us with the experiences, sensibilities, and perspectives of Christ. The exercises culminate in a focused compassion practice, though Ignatius uses the word *love* for what we are calling compassion. This final exercise is his "Contemplation to Attain Love."

The "Contemplation to Attain Love" gathers all that has filled the preceding exercises and points us toward an active, engaged stance of compassionate love in and for the world. Ignatius's complete guidelines for the practice are more detailed and more dense than necessary for our understanding of his process. Boiling them down to three broad movements, three core invitations, can be fruitful:

- **Recollecting Love.** The first broad movement asks us to recall a thing we know to be true: Love is a mutual relationship of communicating needs and of giving. This stage focuses our attention, our thoughts, and our memories on the core concern of the life of faith: compassionate love.

  This movement is a form of recollection (though Ignatius doesn't call it that), a way of remembering, gathering, and focusing all the movements of our being on the thing that is most vital. Teresa of Avila asked us to focus our recollection on Divine Presence itself. Ignatius directs us to the essence of that Presence, which is love.

• **Imagining Divine Conversations.** The second movement
invites us to turn our imaginations toward God. We are to compose a scene in our imagination in which we are standing in the
presence of God, the saints, and the angels. We are to talk with
them about all the good God has given to us and to the entire
universe. (In my own imagination, this is like a panel of experts
being interviewed on a television news show.) At the end of the
conversation we are to offer back to God all that God has given
us. The only thing we keep is the relationship of love and grace
God has with us.

For Ignatius, the more we engage and explore images and
the feelings that accompany them, the more the experience of
our relationship with God increases. In fact, in this practice,
the scene I compose in my imagination eventually carries my
experience without my own effort; the images draw me more
and more deeply into an experience of intimacy with Divine
Presence. Images are so powerful for many of us (especially the
image-filled techno-world most of us inhabit) that Ignatius's
way may seem obvious, normal. But think for a moment how
this approach contrasts with Centering Prayer. In that approach,
as images decrease, the experience of God's presence increases.
Centering Prayer banks on images being cleared away, trusting that images can't adequately portray God. Ignatius, on the
other hand, depended on a richness of images, believing that the
expansion and deepening of our human experience grow intimacy with God.

• **Bringing Love to Life.** Finally, the third broad movement
invites us to a stance of active, compassionate love in the world.
Here Ignatius asks us to have a conversation with God about
how to gather our interior experience of love and apply it in our
lives. For Ignatius, love is not real until our lives become love in
the world. After all, Ignatius created his spiritual exercises to
help people discern vocations for living Divine love in the world.
Ignatius wanted to free us to love without limitation. Nothing
short of that engaged stance of compassionate love for all creation will do.

The Christian tradition teaches that the route to compassion begins with God. Resting in Divine Compassion, we turn to offer compassion to ourselves. Once we find healing and wholeness there, the compassionate impulse invites us out into the world as agents of God, bearers of compassion—first for those dear to us and then for those we find difficult.[22]

Over the centuries, spiritual sages have created a storied legacy of practices designed to help Christians cultivate aspects of the compassionate life. Of course, as our tradition tells us, the way of compassion brings us to places that will challenge us to our core. Jesus walked the compassionate path, and it cost him his life. Compartmentalized practices ill equip pilgrims for the compassionate road. Fortunately, there is a holistic practice to help us on our way. We will explore that practice in chapter 5.

Review and Practice

The practices we've engaged in within this chapter focus directly on growing compassion toward others and include the following:

- **Those Who Are Dear to Us.** The medieval writings referred to as *Meditations on the Life of Christ* ask us to imagine ourselves into the experiences of Jesus' disciples and his mother during his crucifixion. By guiding us to imagine ourselves with them, gazing on the suffering Jesus, the *Meditations* sparks feelings of compassion in us for these people we care about—both those who follow Jesus and Jesus himself.
- **Those We Experience as "Enemies."** The *Meditations* asks us to imagine viewing Jesus' tormentors through his own eyes. The writing guides us into a sharing of Jesus' feelings of compassion toward those who are behaving as his enemies. The author of the *Meditations* seems to know that compassion does not easily flow toward those causing pain. We need a boost. That boost comes from experiencing what Jesus experiences. The author assumes that because we love Jesus, our hearts will soften as we imagine ourselves more and more intimately connected with him. Jesus has offered us compassion when we least expect it and when we

need it the most—even when we have acted like enemies in the world. As a result, our armor of antagonism dissolves, and we join him in compassionate love toward others who have acted as we too often do.

- **Everything in the Universe.** Ignatius of Loyola's "Contemplation to Attain Love" invites us to imagine a conversation with God and divine beings in which we consider all the wonders that flow from God's compassionate love. In conversation with this gathering of divine figures, we come to see the universe from their expansive vantage point, rather than from our narrow perspective. Here we are taking an imaginative step back from the details in our lives to look at the big picture, the God's-eye view. Compassion naturally arises from this perspective. Perhaps the closest real-life analogy comes from astronauts who describe having their perceptions of humankind changed as they view our common home from space. The compassion that emerges from this vantage point doesn't focus only on specific situations and people. Nor does it contain only understandings or only feelings or only actions. No, this divinely-grounded Compassion is a combination of understandings, feelings, and actions. It engages, abides, endures, and expands, encompassing not only those dear to us and our enemies but also all people and even the entire universe.

These compassion-for-others practices expand compassion to encompass wider and wider circles, from people who are dear to us, to those we find to be difficult, to the entire universe, including people we have never met and parts of creation we have never seen. The practices extend the circle of compassion by fully using the Compassion Capacities—imagination, intimacy, and feelings.

Those who developed these practices knew that understanding the nature of compassion or the call to compassion was not enough. They realized our minds, our bodies, and our beings go "all in" only when our ability to create mental pictures links with our ever-present emotions and our natural inclinations for close relationships. In the soil of imagination, feelings, and intimacy, compassion takes root, grows, and flourishes.

Exercises to Cultivate Compassion for Others

The following two exercises are drawn from processes within the Compassion Practice, which we will explore in chapter 5. Each one activates and strengthens our muscles of imagination, intimacy, and feeling in contemporary reflections of the practices we have explored in this chapter. The first one asks us to consider persons dear to us. The second invites us to consider someone we may experience as more difficult. We will wait until chapter 5 to explore exercises that cultivate compassion for people we experience as enemies.

COMPASSION FOR SOMEONE DEAR TO YOU

- Focus on a family member or loved one for this exercise. Imagine that person involved in a behavior or experiencing an impulse or emotion that feels difficult.
- More fully activate your imagination by answering the following questions. It may be necessary to use your imagination and to speculate.

  (Important note: If you find yourself reactive or activated in any way whatsoever, notice that with curiosity, then invite the activated emotion, judgment, or impulse to relax so that you can observe and reflect on this family member.)

  Paying Attention: Describe nonjudgmentally what you see about this family member as you observe the person's experiencing the difficult feeling, impulse, or behavior.

  ▲ What is the person's appearance? Describe this person's clothes, hair, expression.
  ▲ What is the person's behavior?
  ▲ What does the person seem to be feeling?
  ▲ What else might the person be experiencing in this situation?
  ▲ What else might be going on in the person's life that contributes to what is happening?

Understanding Empathically: Using your imagination if necessary, sense what may be the deeper suffering underneath this person's behavior.

- ▲ Fears: What might the person fear?
- ▲ Longings: For what might the person most deeply long?
- ▲ Aching Wounds: What persistent and sensitive wounds may this person carry that exacerbate the pain of the person's situation?
- ▲ Gifts Stifled: What gifts may the person have that are being frustrated or denied now?

- • Summarize your sense of this person's experience by filling in the following. If this person's behavior were a cry of suffering, it would say:
  - ▲ "Please understand (this about me)
  - ▲ I ache for . . . .
  - ▲ Right now I most need . . . ."

- • Write a prayer to whatever sacred presence is significant for your family member, a prayer that expresses what he or she would most deeply want the sacred to know about his or her pain, longings, or deepest needs. (If the family member is not religious, write it to someone, either living or dead, who is a healing and sacred presence in this person's life.) Write the prayer in the first person from this person's perspective. The prayers are confidential; you will not read them to anyone; feel free to express whatever feels right to you.

COMPASSION FOR SOMEONE YOU EXPERIENCE AS DIFFICULT

- • If there is someone who easily comes to mind as a difficult person in your life, think about that person. Recall the person in a situation in which you noticed how difficult this person is. Imagine yourself as fully present in the scene.
- • More fully activate your imagination by answering the questions under "Paying Attention" below. Feel free to embellish the details using your imagination.

(Important note: If you find yourself reactive or activated in any way whatsoever, simply notice this with curiosity, then invite the activated emotion or judgment or impulse to relax so that you can simply observe and reflect on this scenario.)

Paying Attention: Describe nonjudgmentally what you might see about this person.

- ▲ What is the person's appearance?
- ▲ What is the person's behavior?
- ▲ What does the person seem to be feeling?
- ▲ What else might the person be experiencing in this situation?
- ▲ What else might be going on in the person's life that contributes to what is happening?

Understanding Empathically: Using your imagination if necessary, sense what may be the deeper suffering underneath the behavior. (Note: this is not a matter of correctly imagining exactly what the suffering is. Rather, this is an exercise in forming compassion in you in response to suffering, no matter what that might be.)

- ▲ Fears: What might the person fear?
- ▲ Longings: For what might the person most deeply long?
- ▲ Aching Wounds: What persistent and sensitive wounds might this person carry that exacerbate the pain of this person's situation?
- ▲ Gifts Stifled: What gifts may this person have that are being frustrated or denied at this moment?

* If the person's behavior was a cry of suffering, imagine what it would say (by completing these sentences):
  - ▲ "Please understand (this about me) . . .
  - ▲ I ache for . . .
  - ▲ Right now I most need . . ."

* Draw your attention to yourself. What do you notice in yourself in response to these cries?

CHAPTER 5

A Compassion Practice for Our Time

The previous chapter began with the story of my friend Frank Rogers searching for a parking space. Though he was confronted with an angry, aggressive man wielding a rake as if it were a weapon, Frank mitigated the power of his instincts. Instead of lashing out or fleeing, he tapped into the deep, often-hidden stream of Compassion that flows within Frank and all of us. Frank went to his "enemy" and talked with him in a way that helped them both honor the humanity in each other. They spoke with each other in genuine understanding and empathy and came to see themselves in each other, fathers who wanted the best for their children. Compassion begat compassion.

It turns out there is a sequel to Frank's story. The flow of compassion didn't stop with Frank and his new friend. Their interpersonal compassion had an impact beyond their new relationship. Frank encouraged his new friend to take his parking concerns to the city council, and the man did, adding his voice to others with similar concerns. The result? Months later the street was zoned for residents' parking only, and the city created a large parking lot specifically for park visitors.

To be sure, a friendship between former antagonists and the development of a new parking lot are not world-shaking changes. But just as surely, harmful conflicts, even wars, have arisen from disagreements smaller than the one between Frank and his friend. Without compassion, the tiniest conflict can spiral out of control. Only with compassion comes the understanding, honoring, caring, and mutual help that will encompass ourselves, individuals close at hand (both dear and difficult), and those beyond our limited personal contacts. A cascade of compassion can begin with the focused effort of a single individual.

Frank's story gives us a real-world example of what this process looks like in the Christian tradition: Compassion is complete only when compassionate thinking and feeling flow into compassionate action—for ourselves, for other individuals, and even for the systems and structures of the communities and organizations that define our lives together. But how do we form such deep and expansive compassion? How do we (as Frank did) move from scatter-shot 3F reactivities (flight-fight-freeze) to wise, transformative compassion?

I've asked this question again and again throughout these pages. In response, I've shown how a variety of different practices help cultivate compassion. But however profound the practices may be, each contributes to compassion-formation in only a limited way.

Some of the practices highlight being grounded in an experience of receiving Compassion: Desert Prayer, Recollection, and Centering Prayer, for example. Others focus on self-compassion: the Jesus Prayer. And still others highlight compassion for others, as well as for all creation: *Meditations on the Life of Christ* and "Contemplation to Attain Love." More extended processes, such as the thirty-day retreat of the Ignatian Spiritual Exercises, draw together several of these dimensions through a combination of practices. But no single practice from Christian history explicitly leads us through the entire process of compassion cultivation, from being grounded in Divine Compassion to acting compassionately toward ourselves and others. This kind of comprehensive process is exactly what we need, if we truly are to live into the compassion Jesus invites us to embrace.

Fortunately, a comprehensive, integrative compassion-forming practice has recently been developed that meets this need. It draws on historical roots and follows the circle of compassion shaped by Jesus' invitation to love: grounding in Divine Compassion; offering compassion to yourself; offering compassion to others. This practice, the Compassion Practice, moves us from compassionate understandings and feelings to wise, restorative, compassionate actions. It draws wisdom from contemporary research in psychology, neuroscience, and spirituality. In other words, it gathers into one package key compassion-cultivating processes from Christian traditions and from current understandings that lie outside of religious traditions.

We will be exploring the entire scope of the Compassion Practice in this chapter. But to enter the practice as fully as possible, it will help to first look at the two spiritual processes that lie at the heart of the practice. One is a process of working with our interior movements. The second is a process of grounding in Divine Compassion. Both have roots in the historical practices we've explored. We'll begin with the process of working with interior movements.

Working with Interior Movements

The Christian tradition affirms that the essence of God is compassion and that we are to live in response to a Divine invitation to become the compassionate image of God in all we do and are. But that is easier said than done, and the doing of it involves working closely and intentionally with the dynamics of interior lives. We have broadly touched on the dynamics of the interior life in our explorations of the 3F state (in chapter 2). Now we'll take a more detailed look at this ever-shifting terrain to see how the Compassion Practice helps us navigate the path to compassion.

The Compassion Practice draws on an understanding of our inner lives that views experience as comprised of many interior movements or inner motions—the various feelings, thoughts, imaginings, physical sensations, memories, and internal voices that run through us in every moment.[1] If you are like me, you know that each of these interior movements can seem like it has a life of its own.

One of the most vivid memories I have of an interior movement taking control comes from a time when I was twenty years old and studying in England. My student digs were quite spare—a cold, eight-foot square boarding-house room with a bed, a desk, a chair, and a wall heater that only worked when I fed it coins. I was allowed two showers per week. In retrospect, this seems a bit harsh. But for a Hoosier farm boy who had never been out of the United States, anything in England was an exotic paradise.

One evening when I was sitting at my desk in Oxford studying religion (and fully reveling in the fact that I was sitting at my desk in Oxford studying religion), I suddenly broke out in a cold sweat. My heart started racing. I was terrified but for no apparent reason. I loved where I was! Nothing could be better! Still, the feeling of fear was so intense that I had to stop what I was doing and pay attention to what was happening with me. I tried to become still and aware of myself and my surroundings.

Then I faintly heard it. From another student's room several floors below me, came the recorded strains of a slow piece of music played by an orchestra. Harmless, right? That's what I kept telling myself. But the panic persisted. It took me several minutes of paying close attention and pondering the situation to realize why I was having such a reaction.

A couple of years before, as part of a hazing week in the college fraternity I had naively joined, upperclassmen had played the piece of music I later heard in Oxford to first-year students as we stood isolated and blindfolded in the middle of the night in a cold, dark room. As I stood there, terrified, I was told the name of the piece, followed by these threatening words: "Never forget this music. *Never forget this.*"

Two years later, I had assumed I'd forgotten the music. Clearly, some part of me had not. There was still a terror within me, a movement of fear. It didn't matter that I was safe and sound at a wonderful time in my life; I was taken over by an interior movement that functioned beyond my conscious awareness.

It turned out that the interior movement holding me was easily addressed. Once I identified it and fully understood what was happening, I relaxed. The racing heart and cold sweat disappeared. But for people who have suffered horrible trauma, such reactions to triggering events are not so easily wiped away.[2] Panic can overtake them. Physical and emotional reactions can overwhelm them. There is a huge range of reactions between the kind of small reactivity I had in my room decades ago and the debilitating reactivities suffered by, say, soldiers who have returned from war zones. But the same neurophysiological chains of reactions are at work, whether in large or small ways.

Perhaps small versions of these reactions fill your life, like mine: my suddenly swerving the car when a guy cuts me off in traffic; my flash of rage that he gets ahead of me; my boundless glee when he gets pulled over by the police; my shame when I realize that's not very compassionate; my horror that I'm every bit as mean as the guy who cut me off; my thanks that people who admire me can't see how awful I am; my strident self-scoldings to be a better person, more like Jesus; and my continued secret reveling in the fact that I beat the guy to the off-ramp after all.

Each of these interior movements (and all their cousins in the many versions of the 3F states we looked at earlier) can rule my life for a moment or for a lifetime. Something as seemingly inconsequential as my reactions in my student digs those many years ago could have had long-lasting consequences. If the source of my reactive physical symptoms hadn't been so obvious, so easy to recognize, maybe this beautiful piece of music would still torment me. However, most of the reactive interior movements in my life are not so easily addressed. That is where the Compassion Practice comes in.

Before we go on, it's important to note that the Compassion Practice is not the only process that addresses the reactivities of the inner life. You may be familiar with one or more popularized meditation techniques meant to mitigate the potentially debilitating effects of interior movements. But the way the Compassion Practice addresses inner movements is counterintuitive for some of us, or at least it doesn't match the ways many of us have been instructed in how to handle difficult interior movements.

To clarify how the Compassion Practice treats inner movements, I want to look first at what it does not do. That is, I want to show how other practices handle inner movements. Here, for example, is a simplified mash-up of many versions of popularized instructions for how to handle the surge of difficult emotions and thoughts that come to me when somebody cuts me off in traffic and I have a chance to pull over to regroup through a spiritual practice:

> Take a deep breath. . . . Allow your mind to rest, focusing on no thought or feeling. . . . If a thought or feeling comes to you, simply notice it and name what it is. . . . Is it fear? . . . Anger? . . . Something else? . . . Simply name it. . . . And then let it go. . . . Let it drift by and away . . . until it is gone . . . , allowing your mind to rest, unfocused, . . . until another thought or feeling emerges. . . . Notice and name that . . . , and allow it to drift away as well.[3]

Notice the flow of my mashed-up meditation instructions, above. They guide us to let every thought or feeling "drift away until it is gone." They help us finally clear away every interior movement. This process of clearing assumes that interior movements such as thoughts and feelings interfere with spiritual growth. They are impediments on the spiritual path. We are better off without them. No matter how positive they might seem (a beautiful scene in our imaginations, a happy thought), within the spiritual practice they are all barriers, distractions, mental and emotional clutter that keep us from something vital. When they are cleared away, there is room for the true goodness (emptiness? calm? clarity? inner stability? connection with Divine Presence?) that awaits.

Spiritual traditions offer many perspectives on the clearing of inner movements. My composite meditation example above shows one perspective. It encourages us to let inner movements dissipate, clearing away by themselves, which will happen if we surrender control over them and refuse to focus our attention on them. The interferences will most easily clear away if we use a process of gentle, non-grasping, open awareness.

A second perspective on clearing away inner movements shows up in the ancient Desert Prayer, which you may remember from chapter 2. The desert sages repeated a verse from Psalms without ceasing. This flood of sacred words cleared away thoughts, feelings, and images by crowding them out so that they didn't interfere with the sages' relationship with God. This approach, like many others from a variety of religious traditions, teaches that inner movements must be fought, overcome, eliminated—sometimes with rather violent vigor. For example, some ancient monks were taught that thoughts of temptation were to be "dashed . . . against the rock of Christ."[4]

A third perspective on clearing inner movements is subtler than the other two and a bit harder to explain. I'll use a ballgame metaphor to describe it. Think of a spiritual practice in terms of throwing a ball. You get rid of the ball by acting in a certain way—moving your arm and opening your hand. In this metaphor, the ball is the feeling or thought you are wanting to clear away during your spiritual practice. The more you practice moving your arm and opening your hand in just the right way, the stronger and steadier your arm and hand muscles become and the easier it is to get rid of the ball in the way you intend. Professional baseball pitchers depend on this, as do all players of games that involve releasing held spherical objects—boccie ball, tennis, even children's games of dropping marbles into cups. In all of these, life gets better (in terms of the game you're playing) the better you become at getting rid of the ball, clearing it away from you. Not only that, but the more you practice, the stronger your "clearing" muscles get and the easier your intended purpose becomes—whether that means hitting the strike zone with the baseball or the inside of the cup with the marble.

Many spiritual practices take this muscle-strengthening perspective on clearing away inner movements. For instance, you may recall that in Centering Prayer, every time you become aware that you are engaged in something other than being open and available to Divine Presence, you repeat your sacred word to remind yourself of your intention to be available. In this way, your intention clears interior movements away from you; intention is like a spiritual arm releasing the ball of emotion that you want to get rid of. As your intention releases that ball of emotion again and again, your intention gets stronger and stronger. Paradoxically, if you didn't have to deal with those pesky inner movements, your intention wouldn't become so strong; the need to clear away the inner movements is what gives your intention the chance to build muscle so that you can become more and more available to Divine Presence— which is the point of the practice. As you might suspect, other practices build other spiritual muscles. The mashed-up meditation instructions, above, for example, might be used to strengthen awareness: "If a thought comes to you, notice it." Do that again and again, and your *awareness* muscle will grow. Or another section of those meditation instructions might help you surrender control over whatever comes to mind: "Let the thought drift by and away. . . until it is gone." Repeat this over and over, and you'll buff up your spiritual muscle of *surrender*.

These perspectives on clearing interior movements can be helpful, as many traditions of spiritual practice have shown. There may be times in your life when focusing on a practice that takes one of these approaches is exactly what you need. In fact, as you'll see, some of the processes within the Compassion Practice use clearing approaches to strengthen certain spiritual muscles that need honing.

In its entirety, however, the Compassion Practice does not ask you to clear away interior movements. Quite the contrary, for it invites you to deeply, expansively engage and explore these movements. The Compassion Practice does not view interior movements as interfering distractions or enemies to be battled as some traditions do. Nor does it use them primarily to strengthen spiritual muscles, as in other traditions. Instead, it follows those Christian spiritual traditions that view the interior movements as vital, necessary pathways to Divine Presence. The Compassion Practice guides you to engage, explore, and empathically understand inner movements instead of clearing them away.

In our look at spiritual practices from Christian history, we've seen examples of processes that help us to engage and explore interior movements rather than to clear them. We can recall how *Meditations on the Life of Christ* invites us to notice what we are feeling and imagining and to engage those inner movements to expand our experience of compassion. We also can remember how Teresa of Avila's practice of Recollection gathers the interior movements into collective focus instead of clearing them. In these practices, our thoughts, feelings, and imaginings serve as openings to a deeper connection with Divine Compassion.

This exploratory approach to inner movements connects with an ancient theological perspective that sees all interior movements as essentially good, created by God to love God and all creation. According to the influential medieval theologian, Thomas Aquinas, even the most negative emotion or thought began with a longing for God, a true goodness trying to unite with Divine Love. Something has diverted this interior movement from its course or twisted its shape along the way. But still, its essence is goodness aiming for the Divine Good (even as it misses the mark).

In this view, spiritual practices aren't ultimately vaccines meant to eliminate the virus of difficult interior movements, brooms to sweep away the distractions, rivers of goodness to wash away the bad stuff, or weapons for defeating inner enemies. Instead, as Aquinas taught, spiritual practices bring inner movements back into harmony with their true core intentions and into balance with all the other movements the practices work to harmonize.[5]

At this point I want to pause and note how helpful—even revolu-tionary—this view of interior movements is for forming compassion. For decades, I thought that the only legitimate way to handle negative emo-tions and thoughts was to clear them away, as I've described above. But one day several years ago, I was teaching with my friend and colleague Frank Rogers when I heard him say something that radically changed my spiritual path:

> The negative emotions, thoughts, and sensations are not prob-lems. In fact, they are not negative at all. Yes, they are difficult. But that is exactly what makes them so valuable. After all, where did Jesus hang out? With the poor, the troubled, the ill, the out-casts—all the people in the parts of society who were consid-ered difficult, problematic, negative influences. That is where we find the Presence of Divine Compassion—in the shadowed places we tend to want to ignore or cover up. Jesus took compas-sion to those parts of the world. Jesus calls *us* to take compas-sion to those parts of the world. And *that includes the parts of our interior lives that are wounded and troubled and difficult to deal with.* Those are the parts of us that need compassion. Instead of clearing away the difficult movements, we are invited to find ways to offer them compassion. As that happens, we will begin to experience compassion from the inside out. That is what makes these difficult emotions gifts.[6]

Negative emotions, thoughts, and sensations are *gifts?* These com-ments rocked my spiritual world. I had spent inordinate amounts of effort in prayer and meditation for over thirty years trying to get rid of those distracting, problematic, interior movements. In fact, most of my time in contemplative practices had been spent devising strategies for clearing away the difficult movements instead of entering the contem-plative prayers themselves. And in retreats I had attended, teachers had spent long sessions offering techniques that might help me move past these problematic inner dynamics so that I could get to the good stuff.

The perspective of the Compassion Practice turned all of that on its head. It freed me to welcome those difficult interior movements. Now I can see each one's arrival as an opportunity for a great adventure, a chance to explore new, unknown, edgy territory—the X-Games of the interior life. After all, I have explored parts of the external world that I tend to see as challenging, including El Salvadoran barrios in the revolutionary era of the early 1980s, a refugee camp in a Hezbollah-held portion of Beirut, a Beqaa Valley town five miles from Syria's war zone, San Quentin prison, and impoverished villages in Palestine.

I've welcomed the chance to go to all those "difficult" places and others. I've seen these opportunities as gifts to help me gain a more knowledgeable, appropriately compassionate perspective on those distressed parts of the world. So why not approach the parts of my inner life in the same way I approach parts of the external world? Why not bring this same stance of empathic curiosity, willingness to learn, desire to understand, and appropriate compassion to the movements of my interior life, whether easy or difficult? Why not, indeed. I have discovered that this stance, foundational for the Compassion Practice, can free me for a life of compassion in ways I'd never dreamed possible.

The Gift of Interior Movements

Some time ago I visited my good friend Allen, who has been retired from the parish ministry for several years. Every congregation he served loved him, cared for him, and embraced him as a brilliant preacher and gifted pastor. Even now, when the opportunity arises, he blesses people with his pastoral and preaching skills. But these days the primary way he blesses others is by surrounding them with beauty. He has filled the wooded acres around his house with works of art he has created: small writing cottages, a shingled chapel complete with a working bell in the steeple, paintings hanging on fences in tree-sheltered alcoves, sculpted gates opening to hedgerow paths, cairns of flat stones, and outdoor rooms with views of flowers, sunsets, and songbirds. Allen loves beauty. Allen creates beauty. He scatters it around and helps it grow, and he welcomes people to revel in the beauty he creates.

Given Allen's eye for all things beautiful, I was not surprised to see his penchant for beauty show up in every part of his life, including his car. Here's what happened: When I borrowed his car one day, I noticed a piece of black tape on the dashboard. This seemed odd; it was rather inelegant and, well, not very beautiful. But a closer looked showed me that the smooth black strip was hiding something that was worse than the crude appearance of the tape: An orange warning light glowed ominously behind that stuck-on black strip. John hadn't liked the look of that light, so he had covered it. It was not at all beautiful, it looked like trouble, and so he cleared it from sight.

You see the problem—and it wasn't the light. No, the problem was in *ignoring* the light. In the name of beauty, to avoid having to look at something annoying and troubling, Allen had covered something meant to help him keep the car in good working order. And, in fact, the next time I visited Allen, the tape was gone—along with the car, which had died. The broken bits flagged by that ugly warning light had finally taken their toll, causing irreparable damage to the engine.

I confess that I understand all too well why Allen covered that warning light. I'm also inclined to treat the movements of my interior life in similar ways. As I've noted above, there are appropriate, helpful reasons and processes for clearing away difficult inner movements—but fearful, continual avoidance is not one of them. And I, unfortunately, tend toward fearful avoidance. My love of the blessings of beauty, my aversion to things ugly, troubling, annoying, disturbing, or negative, can lead me to avoid movements within that are not pleasing, not beautiful, not attractive, and not easy. I see them as threats or problems instead of what they really are: gifts. They are gifts because they point me to the broken places within myself, the places that need rebalancing and healing, the parts of myself that need compassionate attention.

The Compassion Practice invites us intentionally and boldly to embrace all interior movements as gifts. No matter how troubling these movements may seem, they actually serve as vital signposts toward healing.[7] This stance can free us to new possibilities for compassion.

But taking this stance, understanding this truth, may not get us very far down the path to compassion. Instead, we also need practical processes for engaging these movements. We need to know what to do with these gifts, how to receive them and open them. We need strategies for welcoming them, examining them, and understanding their purposes for our lives if we want to receive their benefits. With that in mind, let's look at how the Compassion Practice invites us to work with our interior movements in ways that lay the foundation for self-compassion and compassion for others.

Tending Interior Movements

When our older daughter, Hannah, was born, I had just begun to write my doctoral dissertation. My wife and I were splitting a pastoral position; I was one-quarter time and she was three-quarters time. The plan: I was to be home writing most days, which meant that I would be doing most of the daytime parenting. *No problem*, we thought. *I'll get a lot done, and quickly, since babies sleep all the time.* Rookie mistake. The dissertation took six years because I quickly learned that I couldn't simply ignore Hannah when she wanted attention.

My on-the-job, new-parent training taught me that ignoring Hannah only made things worse for both of us. If Hannah started to fuss and I kept writing, the fuss turned into a cry, which turned into a scream. If she exhausted herself into sleep by screaming (something I gritted my teeth to allow to happen approximately one time), it turned out that the wet diaper that initially sparked her fussing caused painful chapping, which required more care than changing the diaper immediately would have. As for me, as soon as she started fussing, the last thing I could do was focus on writing. All I wanted to do was pick her up and soothe her. I told myself I *had* to get this writing done; it would be better for all of us in the long run—but to no avail. I couldn't focus. She was in distress. It was a lose-lose situation.

I've since come to understand that mental distractions and chapped skin aren't the only problems that come from inappropriate responses to infants' distress signals. Attachment studies in psychology have shown that relationship styles are deeply affected by the way caregivers interact with babies in the earliest stages of their lives; ignoring a baby in distress can lead to an inability to form healthy relationships in adulthood. (By the way, to Hannah's credit, she has recovered quite nicely from any damage I might have done.) In other words, both short-term and long-term problems grow when caregivers do not appropriately address an infant's immediate needs.

I tell this story not as a confession of my parental shortcomings (which I reserve for my daughters) but to illustrate the way the Compassion Practice works with difficult interior movements, whether they are thoughts, feelings, imaginings, fantasies, conversations in my head, or physical sensations. Through the lens of the Compassion Practice, I have come to think of each challenging inner movement as an infant crying out to let me know it has an unmet need. The cry is not a problem; it is a gift. It's a life-saving reaction built within us like the flight-fight-freeze reactions. I think of it as the signal, the warning light that tells me something within me is broken, wounded, or out of balance and needs help before I break down. Like baby Hannah crying out as I tried to ignore her, that noisy inner movement may not be able to communicate its needs in words. Instead, the cry itself is the communication. It tells me that some aspect of the complex system of living, breathing, embodied consciousness that is my entire self needs care. The inner cry is the emotional parallel of the pain that happens when I burn my hand. It gives me an opportunity to pay attention to that distressed part of me and determine what it needs to heal. It gives me a chance to offer myself compassion. I'm not to treat that cry as a distraction; I'm to tend it with all the love I have within me—just as I did with Hannah those many years ago.

When I notice that some inner movement keeps crying out and when I pay attention to it to better understand it, I am nurturing a caring relationship with it. In other words, I am offering compassion to that part of myself. What's more, as I do that, I'm strengthening my compassion muscle, which helps me offer compassion to whomever needs it—even people I may experience as enemies.

Following the "FLAGs"

So far, in describing the Compassion Practice's approach to movements of the inner life, I've used a variety of metaphors: gifts to open, fussing babies, warning lights on a car dashboard, and pain-transmitting nerve endings. The Compassion Practice adds yet another image to the list: FLAG. This practice invites me to see each of my interior movements as a flag waving at me, signaling that there's something within me that needs my loving attention for healing, freeing, harmonizing, and restoring.[8]

Fortunately (yes, fortunately!) I have internal flags waving at me all the time, asking for (often demanding) my attention. A memorable example of how that works for me happened years ago when I was supposed to present a program proposal to an academic colleague. I was recommending that seminary education be based on contemplative practice. I was extremely anxious about presenting my vision to this colleague. Why? To put it bluntly, I felt as if this man were my enemy. I assumed he would attack or ridicule me in some way because he had a history of doing so. He never had a good word to say about anything I did in my work. He always spoke about it as unfit for a graduate school because it wasn't scholarly enough. My internal flags waved wildly and without pause: first, the thought that I was simply not competent or strong enough to present to someone so knowledgeable and mean; then, the upset stomach the morning of the presentation; finally, the spontaneous wish-fantasy that my car wouldn't start, making it impossible for me to get to the lecture. Each of these inner movements—these gifts, these blessings— alerted me to the fact that there was something within me that needed compassionate attention. Without those waving flags, I might have missed an opportunity for more spiritual growth. With them, I received endless chances to explore and transform the root causes of these inner movements, causes that were usually tucked away in my unconscious.

The image of a waving flag helps me see difficult interior movements in a positive light. What's more, the Compassion Practice uses the letters in *flag* as tools for exploring our inner dynamics. FLAG is an acronym for what lies underneath those noisy interior movements:

- Fears that haunt us and limit our freedoms. These may be large or small. They are rooted in some trauma that may be obvious or not.
- Longings for more in our lives and in the life of the world. Perhaps we've yearned to follow a vocational path but never had the chance to explore it. Or maybe we live in a context that feels like prison, and we thirst for freedom.

- Aching wounds that have not healed. Often these are the result of emotional damage from the earliest years of our lives. They may bind us to old patterns and paths that keep our lives from flourishing.
- Gifts denied or stifled. These may be skills we have that we have never had a chance to apply or some other quality in our lives that cries out to expand into the world for the benefit of the world (including ourselves).

Along with the process of grounding in Compassion (which we'll look at shortly), the FLAG process is the critical heart of the Compassion Practice. It's so crucial to the way the practice builds compassion that even before we start working through the steps of the practice itself, it's helpful to focus on the way the FLAG tool works. To do that, let's look more closely at the FLAG-waving scenario I began describing: my anxiety when faced with presenting a program proposal to the colleague who seemed so nasty.

As I've noted, one thing that happened to me was that I started thinking about my incompetence. How incompetent am I? The voice in my head would be happy to tell you in extravagant detail. Some spiritual-practice traditions would see these denigrating thoughts as harmful distractions and would teach strategies for clearing them away. Fortunately, that works for many, many people. Unfortunately, I am unable to learn those clearing processes. But the FLAG process does work for me. Here's what happens when I apply it to my aversion to giving academic lectures:

- I begin by noticing a cavalcade of thoughts voicing their displeasure at my incompetence. The foundational spiritual capacity of *awareness* is active here.
- I envision one of the voices as a small child berating himself for being so stupid and useless he should stay home and hide. The foundational spiritual capacity of *attention* comes into play at this point, along with the compassion capacity of *imagination*.
- I ask this little boy the FLAG questions, below. Initiating a conversation about deeply held feelings activates the Compassion Capacities of *intimacy* and *feelings*.

   ▲ What do you Fear? Or . . .

   ▲ What Longing do you have that is unfulfilled? Or . . .

   ▲ What Aching wound within you is not healed? Or . . .

   ▲ What Gift within you has not had a chance to be offered to the world or to flourish?

- With open, empathic curiosity I attend to whatever answer may come. *Intimacy* and *attention* continue to be highlighted.

- The answer that emerges from this particular version of the process has to do with fear: "I'm afraid. I know they won't like what I say. And it's going to be bad for me. Just like it was for me with my father whenever I gave my opinion." At this point my imagination gives me a decades-old mental picture of my four siblings, my mother, and me sitting around the dinner table, terrified to speak for fear that if we did, we would be verbally attacked by my father no matter what we said.

- Here, my heart goes out to this imagined little boy, the symbol of my anxiety. I feel compassion for him. I want to alleviate his fear. I want to comfort him and tell him he's done nothing wrong and there's nothing to fear; that he's smart and competent, and I won't let him be hurt. My *feelings* are now working at peak output.

Do you see what's happening here? It's the same thing that happened when newborn Hannah fussed and cried while I was trying to write. I automatically wanted to comfort her, care for her. It took everything in me to try to ignore her. But in the end, I couldn't. Neither of us could stand it.

Now I confess that because I was brought up to value behavior that is quiet, contained, and introverted, I get a bit embarrassed by all the feelings, images, and intimacy that the FLAG process evokes. But here's the thing: Scientists now are able to tell us how such processes work, and they *do* work—because our compassion instinct is as deeply ingrained in us as our fight-flight-freeze instincts.[9] Compassion-catalyzing neurochemicals start flowing when we see images of vulnerable people in pain or other distress, particularly if they are children. In response to these images, our entire beings automatically generate intimate, feeling-inspired caregiving. Yes, we are hardwired for compassion to unfold from images, feelings, and intimate interactions, and that makes sense at the most basic level of survival: Our species with its helpless newborns wouldn't survive without the intimate, empathic, nurturing care connected to the compassion instinct.

FLAG's use of imagination, intimacy, and feelings follows the ancient wisdom expressed in Christian compassion-forming practices we've looked at in previous chapters, especially those in *Meditations on the Life of Christ.* The writers of those compassion-forming dramatic scripts knew that if they could get people to imagine someone they cared for suffering, compassion would automatically emerge. They didn't need twenty-first-century neuroscientists to tell them this truth about humankind. The combined force of feelings, intimate connections, and active imagination (the Compassion Capacities) that shows up in the FLAG exercise and the traditions behind it rewire our neural networks, emotions, and entire bodies from the inside out for healing, freedom, and restoration.

Compassion, One Crib at a Time

I've come to realize that one important benefit of the Compassion Practice is that it allows me to build compassion bit by bit, one part of myself at a time. What do I mean by this? The best way to explain is to compare the Compassion Practice to two powerful compassion-forming practices from Buddhism: *metta* ("loving-kindness") and "Instructions on the Sevenfold Causal Sequence."[10]

The first of these two practices, *metta*, begins by inviting you to wish well-being for yourself, then for those people who easily evoke caring feelings in you, then for those you find to be difficult, gradually expanding the circle of concern until it encompasses the entire universe.

"Instructions on the Sevenfold Causal Sequence" uses a similar process, but it doesn't ask you to begin with yourself. Instead, it guides you to focus on feeling compassion for someone you easily care about (your mother, for instance) and then to move to someone you have neutral feelings about, before turning compassionate attention to those who are difficult, ending with the entire universe.

Despite their slight differences, these two practices focus on offering compassion to individuals as one lump sum, a complete person—myself or someone else—rather than focusing on single interior movements within persons. This sort of whole-person compassion practice is quite powerful for many people, as the centuries-old popularity of these kinds of practices shows. But for others, it's not so easy to cultivate self-compassion in one big chunk. I wish I were one of the former, but, alas, I am one of the latter. It's simply easier for me to build compassion for myself by doing it one part at a time.[11] When I try to be compassionate to my entire self in one fell swoop, I get stuck. The enormity of what I face overwhelms me. I become paralyzed by how inadequate, inept, embarrassed, or afraid I feel. It's as if infants in a nursery were screaming at the top of their lungs, and all I can do is stand at the doorway wishing, hoping, pleading for them to feel better.

The FLAG process gives me a strategy for tending to that roomful of crying infants. Whenever one fusses, a flag is raised on its crib, and I tend to whatever it needs. Then I move to the next one. If this image seems odd, you may want to find another for yourself. One may naturally come to you. For example, images of injured pups needing care come to a friend of mine who works in animal-rescue circles. She easily has compassionate conversations with animals in distress. That is the key for FLAG images: they need to easily and automatically evoke a compassionate response in you. For me, images of children in distress do that: compassion, one crib at a time.

The FLAGs of Freedom

I've gone into some detail to emphasize the counterintuitive notion that negative interior movements are mechanisms built into our human nature for our own well-being, and I've laid out a key part of the Compassion Practice—the FLAG process—to show how we can work with difficult interior movements in a way that takes advantage of the help they offer.

But why spend all this time on this process before we even get into the details of the Compassion Practice? What makes it so special? In fact, FLAG is something like a fallback option within the practice; FLAG is an exercise you can return to whenever you get stuck, frustrated, confused, or overwhelmed. It's a route to inner freedom.

In every spiritual practice, there are times when things don't go per-fectly smoothly, when it doesn't follow your expectations, hopes, and desires, and that is true of the Compassion Practice. The FLAG process allows you to face, even welcome, these rough times in the practice. It allows you to be free of the unconscious and conscious requirements and compulsions to have things go in expected, prescribed ways.

When spiritual practices haven't gone easily for me, I've been given a particular kind of instruction over the years: "Just do it again. Try harder. Don't give up." That's a familiar strategy. It's like something my high school basketball coach used to yell at us during our daily practice: "Push *to* the pain and *through* the pain!"

Although that may be the right strategy for Indiana basketball—though I have my doubts since we won only three out of twenty games—I know it doesn't work in the Compassion Practice. Rather than encourag-ing you to ignore difficult interior movements such as physical or emo-tional pain, the Compassion Practice invites you to approach them with these affirmations:

* Interior movements are messages meant to help you compassion-ately find ways to heal, free, and restore your life and the life of the world.
* The "louder" the movement, the more you are invited to attend to it. If an interior movement keeps coming up, interfering with the focus of your practice, tend to that noisy movement. Pray *that*, rather than what you were already focused on.

From these affirmations come strategies for doing the practice when it isn't going exactly as you are expecting, planning, or wanting.

To explore these strategies, let's return to my experience of present-ing a proposal to that colleague who seemed like my enemy. Let's assume I've used the FLAG process on my anxiety for quite a while, but the process doesn't seem finished. So I return to it determined for it to work. I focus again on that anxiety by using the FLAG exercise, hoping to ease my anxiety through offering it compassion. But nothing happens; the exercise is simply not productive. I'm not able to focus on the anxiety at all. I'm stuck. My attention wanders. I feel frustrated. Again I tackle my feelings of anxiety with still no progress, only frustration. And I try again, but nothing happens. Now I'm really feeling frustrated.

At this point my tendency is to push through or ignore the frustration, trying to focus on exploring the original feeling (anxiety) I'd identified. But the Compassion Practice affirms that the loudest, most persistent interior movement is the one that needs compassionate tending. And what is the loudest, most persistent movement now? Frustration. In this case, one interior movement (anxiety) has led to another (frustration), which is the one that needs my attention in this moment. So the practice invites me to turn my attention to the feeling of frustration—to pray *that*—instead of the anxiety. Again, the practice encourages me to follow the movement that is loudest and most persistent. I'm freed from struggling to focus in a way that simply isn't working. Instead, I use the FLAG exercise on the thing that is alive, the thing that's in my face: my frustration.

What would it look like to use the FLAG process on my frustration? Here's an example:

- I ask myself what this feeling of frustration would look like if it were a small child.
- The image of a small child comes to me: a five-year-old boy stomping around a room with arms straight down at his side and fists clenched.
  - ▲ I strike up a conversation with him using FLAG:
  - ▲ Fear: "Are you afraid of something? What is it?"
  - ▲ Longing: "Or are you yearning for something that seems out of reach? What is it?"
  - ▲ Aching Wound: "Or are you feeling the pain of an emotional, spiritual, or physical wound that has not healed? What is it?"
  - ▲ Gift Stifled: "Or is there some good thing you have to offer the world but have not been able to? What is it?"
- The answers I receive to one or more of these questions will shape a conversation with this interior movement. That imaginative, intimate, affective interaction will expand and deepen my natural compassion for the part of myself represented by this interior movement I feel as frustration—and imagine as a storming five-year-old.

It may seem that I'm waving this FLAG a bit too many times, but there's a point to my repetition of the process, and it bears emphasizing. In the Compassion Practice, we don't need to push through the pain. We aren't asked to struggle against the barriers. Instead, the practice invites us to explore the movement that's demanding the most attention. This approach flows from the assumptions I've listed for addressing difficult moments in the practice:

* Interior movements are messages meant to help us compassionately find ways to heal, free, and restore our lives and the life of the world.
* The louder the movement, the more we are invited to attend to it.

This does not mean you flit from one movement to another. Rather, these are to be well-considered shifts; you'll change your focus only when a movement consistently obscures others. You get to apply the FLAG exercise to the movements that naturally accept it, rather than forcing it onto movements that aren't ready. In other words, *you get to respond to places that draw your attention, rather than struggling to avoid them.* Notice that this flows from the affirmations I've listed above: Interior movements are beneficial messages, and the more noticeable they are, the more you are invited to tend to them.

I've found great freedom in this exercise. It's like being given permission to travel to a country I want to explore rather than being forced against my will to visit a place I want to avoid. We can do this again and again whenever the way ahead seems blocked. The FLAG exercise is an essential key to the practice. It's always available to us to open new territory in our interior lives. It will free us to follow our interior movements down the path to compassion.

Grounding in the Presence of Divine Compassion

Having explored one of the core processes within the Compassion Practice—the FLAG exercise—let's turn now to the other core process in the practice: grounding in the Presence of Divine Compassion.

We looked at grounding practices in chapter 2, but grounding in Compassion is worth revisiting. Without this grounding, the 3F states can overwhelm us, and interior movements can capture us and drive our behavior. Without this grounding, a reactive impulse to help others, untampered by self-compassion (which includes wise attention to our own limitations), can trap us. When we attempt to offer more help than we can deliver, sheer exhaustion can set in. This exhaustion—which may turn into apathy and even bitterness—is often referred to as "compassion fatigue." But in such cases compassion is no longer in play. Instead, reactive feelings of empathy drive us—empathy that is not yet refined by the wisdom that flows from Compassion.[12] In these moments, compulsion supersedes the discerning wisdom that turns empathy into genuine compassion. This compulsive "helpful" behavior ultimately causes harm instead of good.

Only when Compassion grounds you can you offer genuine compassion to the crowd of interior voices, feelings, thoughts, and sensations calling for your attention. Only when Compassion grounds you can you offer genuine compassion to the crowds of people in the world who need loving care.

To become grounded in Compassion is to follow Jesus' lead and step away from the crowds—those within you and those in the world—and go off to a quiet place. You may need to make yourself available to the Presence of Compassion for a period—even if only for a moment—to soak in the Divine Compassion that calms you, replenishes you, and frees your own compassion to flow to the crowds that fill you and the crowds that surround you.

Whenever I consider grounding in Compassion I think back to when I held baby Monica, rocking her in the darkness those many years ago. I felt myself being held by Compassion every bit as much as I held Monica.

I suspect that you too have felt such moments, memories you can call to mind—a palpable sense of beauty, peace, safety, or loving presence. Perhaps it came as you noticed a brilliant sunset. Maybe you were gazing on a loved one asleep beside you. Maybe someone brought you a meal and a kind word when you were ill or grieving. Or perhaps you were singing hymns or spiritual songs with a community that holds you dear. I suspect that someplace, sometime, you have experienced at least one moment of being grounded in Compassion. I hope, I trust, this is true for you. We all need such moments.

The Compassion Practice takes as a given this need for grounding in Compassion. As we will see, the practice cannot work if we do not open ourselves to receive the Divine Presence of Compassion. That is true for the beginning, but it is also true at every moment throughout the practice. The practice begins with grounding and returns to grounding again and again. In fact, the practice encourages us to ground ourselves in the Presence of Compassion without hesitation, whenever we feel the need. That is important enough to restate: *During the practice, whenever we feel the need, we are invited to return and to become grounded in Divine Compassion.*

We will turn now to explore how this grounding in Compassion plays out in the Compassion Practice itself. As we work our way through the practice, I invite you to carry the above invitation with you. If this is the only invitation you respond to for much of the time in the practice, it will be enough. The grounding that you find will be what your soul most fully needs.

The Compassion Practice [13]

The overall flow of the Compassion Practice follows Jesus' threefold invitation to love God, self, and others. It moves from an experience of grounding in the presence of Compassion to offering compassion to yourself—so that you may act compassionately toward others. In the Compassion Practice, these three movements are called "Catching Your Breath," "Taking Your Pulse," and "Taking the Other's Pulse." Let's explore the three movements of the Compassion Practice one at a time before putting them back together in a real-life example. The version of the practice we'll use focuses on offering compassion to someone experienced as an enemy.

Catching Your Breath:
Grounding in Divine Compassion

Have you ever been reminded to catch your breath? I remember my kindergarten teacher saying that to me often. She said it to me at school *and* at home, since my kindergarten teacher also happened to be my mother. So, yes, I heard "catch your breath" a lot. It meant that I'd do well to slow down, to take a break, to consider what I was doing, to rest for a moment, and to take stock of myself and the situation.

Of course, that's not how I would have put it when I was six years old. It was enough to hear "catch your breath." No explanation was needed; I got it. Perhaps I was angry because my brother had knocked down my Lincoln Log building. Or maybe I was frustrated because my three sisters were getting more parental attention than I was. (It's hard to be the oldest of five children under seven.) Whatever distressing or stressful thing was happening to me, "catch your breath" usually worked to interrupt the flow of whatever childhood version of a fight-flight-freeze state I was caught up in.

The phrase works like that for me to this day, so I find it to be a helpful beginning point for the Compassion Practice. In fact, it's a user-friendly version of grounding in Compassion. The breath I'm going to catch isn't only mine; it's the Breath of Divine Presence, flowing in, through, and around me and all that is. To catch my breath in the practice is to pause and open myself to the Presence of Compassion in whatever way best fits me. That is why it helps me begin the practice, and it also gives me a way to return to it or to simply rest whenever that is needed.

There are many ways to catch my breath; there are many processes for grounding in the Divine Presence that is Compassion. Here are a few:

- I breathe gently and deeply, noticing each breath as it moves my diaphragm, noting how the Breath of Life is filling and sustaining me and resting in the calm that comes through this breathing.
- Using a version of Teresa of Avila's Recollection, I gently invite my energies, thoughts, imaginings, feelings, and physical sensations to gather in a singular focus on God. I turn the attention of my entire being toward the Presence of Compassion.

* After the fashion of Centering Prayer, I follow my intention to be open to God, using a sacred word to remind myself to be available, and I rest in that receptive state.

* I recall a sacred moment, a moment when I have encountered the Presence of Compassion. It is a time or place in which I experienced great peace, love, security, care, joy, or beauty. Perhaps it involves a person who has cared for me. For instance, I often return to memories of being at my grandmother's house when I was a child. Being there with her brought me a sense of safety and love. In my imagination, I reexperience that moment and rest in it for a time.

* I spend a few moments singing a sacred chant. Having spent a year in a Christian monastic community, I find that gentle chanting moves me easily to a sense of grounding in Compassion.

* I repeat a bit of scripture in the style of the Desert Prayer. The sacred words invoke a sense of God's presence, carrying all my attention toward God. They drown out all else so that I can rest in a sense of being grounded in Compassion.

* I close my eyes and, as slowly as possible, extend my arms out in front of my body, palms up. Then I draw my arms back as slowly as possible to place my hands over my heart. As I move, I keep my mind's eye focused on my hands. I imagine them, seeing them as if I am watching them with my eyes. I might combine this motion with the mantra, "Come, Divine Compassion."

Each of us has unique ways of grounding in Compassion. I've only scratched the surface of possibilities. You may want to explore some for yourself. As you experiment with grounding practices, notice which ones allow you to settle into a stable, quiet alertness in which you feel at ease, peaceful, nonjudgmental—grounded.

Taking Your Pulse: Offering Compassion to Yourself

Most of us know all too well that ungrounded, reactive states pump up our neurophysiological systems. We get flooded with flight-fight-freeze chemicals, so hearts race and breathing quickens. A quick and easy way to get a read on your 3F status in any moment in time is to take your pulse.

The Compassion Practice uses physical pulse-taking as a metaphor for tending your ability to be compassionate. In the practice, "Taking Your Pulse" means to turn your attention to yourself to identify, assess, understand, and offer compassion to the interior movements that may be driving your inclinations and behaviors.

It's important to remember that in the practice you can accurately "Take Your Pulse" only to the extent that you are grounded in the Presence of Compassion. So before you "Take Your Pulse," the practice invites you to enter a grounding exercise called "Catching Your Breath." It invites you to return again and again to ground yourself in Compassion, using processes that include an exercise called "Inviting the Presence of Compassion." Attending so closely to yourself in "Taking Your Pulse" requires the clarity and stability that come through continually soaking in the Presence of Compassion.

The process of "Taking Your Pulse" begins with the FLAG exercise. It moves to an exercise of "Inviting the Presence of Compassion." And it culminates in an action of wisely discerned compassion. To illustrate how this works, I invite you to take another look at what happens when I must present to a colleague who seems like an enemy to me:

- I *Catch My Breath,* grounding myself in Compassion in whatever way fits me. This initial grounding gives me a foundation of clarity, calm, and open curiosity to nonreactively explore whatever emerges. It sets the stage for all that follows.
- I *Take My Pulse.*
  ▲ FLAG
    — Focusing the FLAG questions on my anxiety (as I have described above) brings me an image of a little boy, berating himself for his stupidity. This little boy (the symbol of my anxiety) tells me he is afraid.
    — I notice a feeling of compassion for him, wanting to relieve his pain.
  ▲ I *Invite the Presence of Compassion.* This is a form of grounding in Compassion. It keeps me connected to Divine Presence as I move through the practice.

— I invite the Presence of Compassion to join me with the little boy, this symbol of my anxiety.

— Together we rest in whatever experience Compassion brings us. Perhaps what comes is a version of "Catching My Breath." In any case, what develops is a deepening sense of Divine Compassion combined with a deepening feeling of compassion for the boy before me. Grounding in Compassion expands and intensifies my capacity to feel compassion toward the part of me symbolized by this imagined boy.

▲ *I Act with Wise Compassion* (toward part of myself).

— I ask the imagined boy, "What do you need from me that will ease your pain?"

— I ask of Compassion, "What might I offer this child who needs my compassion?"

— I ask of myself, "What do I have to offer this child who needs my compassion?"

— From the answers that emerge, I act in compassion toward this child, the symbol of my anxiety.

— In this moment and at least once each day for the next week, I will call to mind the image of this child, and I will do so as I prepare to face the colleague who makes me so anxious, my enemy.

— In those times, I will imagine myself rocking this child, the symbol of my anxiety (as I rocked my daughter when she was an infant), offering compassion to this distressed part of me even as I rest in Divine Compassion.

At this point the practice has moved from being grounded in the Presence of Compassion to offering compassion to a FLAG-waving interior movement. This means that the automatic reactivity of my anxiety no longer captures me. The anxiety has been calmed, and in that calming I am free to turn compassion beyond myself.

Settled into the ground of Compassion and having built a foundation of self-compassion, I can now offer genuine compassion to another person, even someone I experience as my enemy.

Taking the Other's Pulse:
Offering Compassion to the Other.

The process of being compassionate to someone you find difficult follows the same path as being compassionate to yourself. The same spiritual muscles are at work. The same spiritual exercises apply. But they are all directed toward your outer world instead of your inner world.

At this point, having "Taken Your Pulse," there's a good chance you'll already have a sense of being grounded in Compassion. If not, you can "Catch Your Breath" again or engage in some other grounding exercise.

In any case, when interior movements are no longer waving flags at you, you are ready to offer compassion to the person who triggered your reactions in the first place. And how do you do that? You use the FLAG exercise, but focus it on your "enemy" rather than on your interior movements. Here's an example of how that might work for me in relation to the colleague who seemed to be my antagonist:

- In my imagination, I turn my attention toward this man.
  - ▲ I ask myself what this person would look like if he were a small child in pain or other distress.
  - ▲ Now the image of a small child comes to me: a three-year-old boy hiding under a table.
  - ▲ I strike up a conversation with him using FLAG questions.
    - — What *fears* do you have? Or . . .
    - — What are you *longing* for? Or . . .
    - — What *aching wounds* do you carry? Or . . .
    - — What thwarted *gifts* do you have?

The answers I receive to one or more of these questions will shape a conversation with the boy who symbolizes my antagonist. That imaginative, intimate, affective interaction will expand and deepen my natural compassion for this him.

- Invite the Presence of Compassion.
  - ▲ I invite the Presence of Compassion to join me with the little boy.

▲ Together we rest in whatever experience Compassion brings us. Perhaps this is a version of "Catching My Breath." In any case, what develops is a deepening sense of Compassion combined with a deepening feeling of compassion for the boy before me. Grounding in Compassion expands and intensifies my capacity to feel compassion toward this imagined boy.

• I act with wise compassion toward the other.

▲ I ask the imagined boy, "What do you need from me that will ease your pain?"

▲ I ask of Compassion, "What might I offer this child who needs your compassion?"

▲ I ask of myself, "What do I have to offer this child who needs my compassion?"

▲ I receive this answer: "I am so afraid everyone will find out I'm not as smart as I appear and that I'm a fraud." Whether this is exactly what the man himself would say is beside the point. The point is to open me to my innate compassion. Based on this answer, I act in compassion toward the child, this symbol of my enemy:

— Whenever I am to meet with my antagonist, I will imagine him as the child who draws my compassion.

— I will take an open, affirming stance with him, rather than a defensive, prickly attitude.

The details I have described above show a version of what happens when I engage in the Compassion Practice. In my description, you see not only the specific steps of the practice but also a look at what those steps can create in thoughts, feelings, and actions—at least in my life. What it forms in your life will probably look nothing like what it created in mine. You will bring your own inner movements, relationship challenges, and social contexts to the practice, and that will make all the difference in how it plays out for you.

The Review and Practice section below lays out key concepts and a detailed outline of the practice. I encourage you to experiment with it by either easing into one portion of it if a slow approach seems best, or by moving through the whole practice one step at a time. Either way, I trust that the Compassion Practice offers a powerful possibility for shaping your life into an active image of Divine Love.

Review and Practice

You can find a more complete description and exploration of the Compassion Practice in Frank Rogers's books, as well as at the end of this chapter. But for now, I want to review the basic structure of the practice and reiterate key points that may be helpful in fully entering into it yourself and in offering it to others.

Here again is the basic structure of the Practice:

1. *Catch your breath.* (Ground yourself in the Presence of Compassion.)
2. *Take your pulse.* (Offer compassion to yourself.)
   a) FLAG exercise with yourself
   b) Grounding in the Presence of Compassion
   c) Acting with wise compassion toward yourself
3. *Take the other's pulse.* (Offer compassion to the other.)
   a) FLAG exercise with the other
   b) Grounding in the Presence of Compassion
   c) Acting with wise compassion toward the other

As you begin to work with the Practice, engaging it more fully through your own unique experiences, it may be helpful to recall these core guidelines and understandings:

- The Compassion Practice follows the path of Jesus' threefold invitation to love: love of God (grounding in Compassion as you Catch Your Breath); love of self (Take Your Pulse); and love of neighbor (Take the Other's Pulse).
- Whenever you experience a sense of being grabbed by some interior movement, pay attention to it. It may warrant further exploration. Consider pausing and doing the FLAG exercise with that inner movement; in other words, pray *that.* Those FLAG-waving

parts of you are vital invitations to self-compassion. Offer your-self compassion one interior movement at a time.

- Remember that you can turn to grounding in Compassion when-ever you feel the slightest need (or any other kind of invitation).
- The Practice particularly uses the "foundational spiritual capaci-ties" in these ways:
  - ▲ *Intention* shows up most fully when grounding in Compassion.
  - ▲ *Awareness* is especially active when noticing FLAG-waving interior movements.
  - ▲ *Attention* comes to the fore in focusing on the images and conversations within the FLAG exercise.
- The Practice particularly uses the Compassion Capacities in these ways:
  - ▲ *Imagination* is especially engaged within the FLAG exercise.
  - ▲ *Intimacy* is active in processes of grounding in Compassion as well as in the relationship that unfolds during the FLAG exercise.
  - ▲ *Feelings* are engaged in virtually every dimension of the Practice.
- The Practice incorporates the various Christian traditions of compassion-forming practices we have explored:
  - ▲ As with Desert Prayer, Recollection, and Centering Prayer, the Compassion Practice grounds us in the Presence of Compassion.
  - ▲ Reflecting the Jesus Prayer's movement to "place the mind in the heart," the Compassion Practice turns us to a divinely grounded self-compassion.
  - ▲ As with the *Meditations on the Life of Christ*, the Practice imaginatively guides us to intimate feelings of compassion for others—not only those dear to us but even those we experi-ence as enemies.
  - ▲ Sharing the sensibilities of "The Contemplation to Attain Love," the Practice invites us to an abiding stance of engaged, active compassion toward all that is.

The Compassion Practice in Two Versions

While the Compassion Practice has the bare-bones structure I've outlined above, it can be engaged in a variety of ways, depending on the needs of the moment. The two versions below give a taste of the many ways we can use the Practice. The first version focuses on compassion for someone we care for naturally. The second attends to someone who seems like an enemy. Both show how the Practice engages the Compassion Capacities—imagination, intimacy, and feelings—to grow compassion for ourselves and for others.

The Compassion Practice for Someone Dear to You

- **Catch Your Breath.** Ground yourself in whatever way is most helpful to you—listen to music; read a sacred text; light a candle; or sit in a settling silence. Take several deep breaths and ease into an interior space that feels safe and grounded. Invite God's presence to hold and sustain you during this practice.
- **Take Your Pulse.** Once you have settled into a grounded interior space, consider some person to whom you feel invited to extend compassion. This can be a loved one, a coworker, a stranger you've encountered during the day, or a person in your community whose suffering moves you.

  Take a moment and turn inward. Notice what interior movements stir within you as you consider the person in your awareness. Welcome and hold any that are there. You might experience pity, fear, anxiety, discomfort at his or her distress, or perhaps measures of your own grief and pain. You may name them in this way: "I see that sadness is here."

  Assure these interior movements that you are aware that they are present for a reason, and if they prove to be tenacious, you will ponder them more fully. Invite them to relax so that you can be genuinely open and attentive to the person in your awareness.

- **Take the Other's Pulse.**
  - ▲ **Paying Attention.** In your imagination, turn your attention toward the person to whom you feel invited to extend compassion. For a few moments, pay attention without judgment to what this person is doing and the way this person is doing it as if your observation goes without notice.
  - ▲ **Understanding Empathically.** While you continue to gaze upon this person, cultivate a deeper understanding of the soulful cry hidden within this person's emotions or behaviors. Use the FLAG questions to cultivate this understanding:
    — What *fears* does this person carry?
    — What *longings* pulsate within this person?
    — What *aching wounds* haunt this person?
    — What is this person's hidden and thwarted *gift* yearning to flourish?"
  - ▲ **Loving with Connection.** Let yourself feel a sense of compassionate connection to this person. Simply love or care for this person just as you would love a wounded or frightened child who needs care.
  - ▲ **Sensing the Sacredness.** If it feels right, notice if the presence of God feels near and invite that presence—as Jesus, Mary, a symbol of the Holy Spirit, the warmth of God's light—to be with this person at the source of this person's suffering, tending this person in whatever way feels healing and restoring.
  - ▲ **Embodying New Life.** Let yourself embrace the new life that yearns to be birthed within the person.
- **Decide What to Do.** Brainstorm various compassionate actions you might embody as they relate to this person. Consider each of the following types of actions and try to list one, two, or even several possible actions under each category.
  - ▲ Acts of Generosity
  - ▲ Acts of Service
  - ▲ Acts of Witness
  - ▲ Acts of Solidarity
  - ▲ Acts of Empowerment
  - ▲ Acts of Justice

▲ Of the various actions that have come to you, be aware of those that most attract, energize, intrigue, surprise, or draw you. Consider that action in light of the signposts of the Compassion Practice:

— Does this action seem to flow from and sustain your own sense of personal and sacred groundedness?

— Does this action promote and preserve the flourishing of your own humanity? Does it flow from your own sense of personal power? Does it maintain and enhance your own human dignity? Does it employ your own unique gifts, skills, and resources? Can you engage in this action without other interior movements or parts of you becoming concerned and activated?

— Does this action promote and preserve the flourishing of the other? Does it maintain and enhance the person's human dignity? Does it meet the person at the source of the person's deepest and most life-giving needs? Does it contribute to the person's own sense of power? Does it invite any appropriate need for accountability and restoration?

▲ After pondering these considerations, discern which action feels most resonate with these signposts. What action do you feel most invited to embody toward this person? Which action feels most right?

▲ As a final consideration, imagine yourself engaging in this act of compassion. Like watching a movie, see yourself speaking the words or undertaking the compassionate action that you feel called to embody. Notice what reactions are stirred up within you, and sense if they resonate with the compassion you feel moved to embody. Notice the effect the action may have on the other person, and sense if it resonates with the compassion you feel moved to embody.

▲ If it continues to feel right, extend this compassion into the future encounter you intend to have with this person. Then embody the action itself.

The Compassion Practice with an Enemy

- **Get Grounded.** Listen to music, read scripture, light a candle, or sit in silence while listening to your own breathing. Offer yourself to the One who continues to love the world into being. Take several deep breaths and ease into an interior silence.
- **Take Your Pulse.**
  - ▲ **Pay Attention.** Allow into your awareness someone who has triggered some form of repulsion within you recently.

    For a moment, imagine this person and the behavior that stirs repulsion within you. In your imagination, ask that person to recede into some sequestered room, away over the horizon, or into the light of the sacred so that you can feel safe from this person's presence and influence right now.

    Turn your attention inward and notice the feeling, sensation, or internal movement this person activated within you. Do not be taken up into its power, nor judge and suppress it. Cultivate a nonjudgmental awareness that this movement is within you.

    You might do this by saying something like, "Anger is here. I see you, anger." You might sense where it is in your body and say, "Tightness in my chest is here. I feel you, tightness."

    If you feel open to understanding this movement more deeply, proceed. If not, then notice what you are feeling instead and invite that feeling to relax.
  - ▲ **Understanding.** Invite this repulsion to surface the wound, secret shame, or stifled gift underlying its intensity. If it is helpful, invite it to express itself as a person (a child, an angel, a frustrated old man) or an object (a hot iron, a hammer). Ask this inner movement or symbol which FLAG questions reveal a deeper understanding and compassion within you.
    — What is your deepest fear?
    — What is your deepest longing?
    — What aching wound still bleeds within you?
    — What hidden gift feels stifled and frustrated at being denied?

- **Love.** Let yourself feel a sense of compassionate connection to whatever part of you surfaces from within. Love or care for this part of you, just as you would love a wounded or frightened child who needs care.
- **Sensing the Sacred.** Invite God, Jesus, the Holy Spirit, or some sacred figure to be with this part of you in whatever way brings healing or gives life.
- **Embracing the New Life.** Notice any new life or perspective that is emerging within you and allow this gift to flow throughout your body and into every part of who you are.
- **Acting.** Sense if there is an invitation for one concrete action you might take to sustain the new life within you and tend to whatever your inner world most needs from you as you step toward life, power, and personal wholeness.
- **Take the Other's Pulse.** Only if it feels right, turn your attention back toward the initial person who activated your repulsion. Notice what this person looks like from this space of grounded connection. If it feels right, extend your compassion or the compassion of God toward this person, beginning with "Pay Attention," below. If it does not feel right, notice that reluctance and assure that part of you that still needs time and space that you will tend it as it needs.
  - ▲ **Pay Attention.** Remember a time when this person was involved in some behavior that triggered you. For a few moments, observe without judgment or reactivity what this person is doing and the particular way he or she is doing it. Watch with an open curiosity like an artist preparing to paint. What does this person look like—what is his or her attire? Facial expression? Body posture? What are the behaviors? Words? Emotions? If what you notice activates you, invite that reaction within you to relax—you are simply paying attention to this person.
  - ▲ **Understanding.** Remember that whatever this person is saying or doing it is rooted in some suffering. This person's behavior is a cry aching to be heard and tended. Cultivate a

deeper understanding of the suffering hidden underneath the behavior by asking yourself the following:

— What seems to be this person's deepest fear?

— What is this person's deepest longing?

— What aching wound is still tender and seems to be stinging this person right now?

— What stifled gift seems to be frustrated and is fighting to be recognized?

▲ **Loving Connection.** If it emerges, let yourself feel a sense of compassionate connection to the suffering underneath the person's behavior, just as you would love a wounded or frightened child who needs care.

▲ **Sensing the Sacred.** Invite God, Jesus, the Holy Spirit, or some divine figure to come and be with this person at the source of this person's suffering, tending this person in whatever way feels healing and restoring.

▲ **Embodying New Life.** Sense the new life that yearns to be birthed within this person and extend your desire for this healing or life to flourish.

• **Discern Compassionate Action.** Sense if there is an invitation for one concrete action you might take to extend compassion toward this person or otherwise embody the grace of this prayer. This may mean having in your mind an image of this person suffering. Or you might carry a symbol of your intention to be with this person from a grounded space. Another possibility is to think of a word or phrase that helps you remember that this person is in God's gracious care when you're there. (For a more complete description of this dimension, see "The Compassion Practice for Someone Dear to You," above.)

THE INVITATION TO COMPASSION

began the previous two chapters with the story of Frank Rogers's encounter with an enemy who became a friend. The movement from enemy to friend depended, for Frank, on working the Compassion Practice. Using imagination, intimacy, and feelings, Frank looked past the man's antagonistic behavior to discover the good intentions of a fearful, protective father. To do that, Frank attended first to his own riled-up interior movements—reactions that also sprang from the good intentions of a fearful, protective father.

The example I gave of my own experience of the Practice followed a path like Frank's. A grounding in Compassion freed me to offer compassion to myself, which freed me to offer it to a professional colleague I experienced as an enemy.

My experience didn't unfold exactly as Frank's did or as anyone else's would. The move from antagonism to compassion is a mysterious, grace-filled process, however it happens. And whatever that sacred move looks like, one thing remains constant: The invitation to embrace true compassion comes to us in every moment of every day of our lives. I am always surprised by how that invitation can sneak up on me—and how difficult it can be to respond to it.

Case in point: A few weeks ago, I bought some small trees to shade and screen our yard. In response to California's drought, my wife and I wanted natives that would grow quickly with little water. I had done the necessary research and found an amazing native-plant nursery a few miles from our house. About a week after I got the small trees home, I started to turn my mind to planting them. It was only then that I realized I'd accidentally taken six plants instead of the five I'd paid for.

That was a very frustrating discovery. I was racing against so many deadlines that I had no spare time to call the nursery and arrange an appointment to return the extra tree to its rightful owner. But being the oh-so-compassionate person I am (since, after all, I was in the midst of writing a book about compassion), I decided I would do what needed to be done to avoid the nursery being ripped off, even though the owner hadn't realized I'd taken an extra tree.

Unfortunately, the only time available for me to meet the nursery owner was a time my wife wanted me to walk our dog so that she could go to a meeting. But I, with my superpowers of compassion, had a compassionate solution! I would take our dog along with me and go directly to the park for a run after the nursery, thus helping the nursery's bottom line, allowing my wife to go to her meeting, exercising our dog, exercising myself, and minimizing my use of planet-warming fuel. Everybody in the whole world wins! Compassion abounds!

Not only that, but on the way to the nursery, I made a sudden, on-a-dime stop to allow a frail, elderly woman to cross the busy street. Mr. Compassion strikes again!

And here's where it gets rocky. That sudden stop-on-a-dime to help the frail, elderly woman? It initiated a chain reaction: the dog slid off the back seat of the car; the dog landed on the tree; the tree broke; the nursery asked for one of the un-broken trees instead of the broken one I showed up with; I had to drive home to get an unbroken tree and drive back; the car used additional gas; the dog had to wait for a shorter walk later in the day; the four extra trips reduced my writing time; the broken tree cost me $50; the 3F state took hold of me; and my wife had to handle "Mr. Compassion" going on a tirade for an hour about what a messed-up morning he'd had and how it's all the fault of trying to be so stinking compassionate and *is the universe conspiring against compassionate people or what?*

Yes, in my experience, the invitation to compassion can happen when you least expect it. Compassion is a relentless teacher. Those noisy interior movements will not be denied.

So I end somewhat as I began—recognizing that being compassionate is hard and understanding that being compassionate toward enemies is extraordinarily hard indeed. Sometimes the enemy is a movement within, a reactive thought, a compulsive feeling. (*I'm terrified! I can't do it! I'm just not smart enough to present this proposal to my colleagues!*)

Or sometimes the enemy is a love-starved soul whose only form of communicating the need for caring contact pushes people away. (Remember ten-year-old Donnie Sherman "attacking" me in the gym at recess?) And sometimes even the whole universe can seem like the enemy, turning our best-laid plans to chaos. (How about an "easy" trip to return a tree?)

The deepest parts of our beings move toward compassion whether the path is easy or not. Fortunately, we are not left to our own devices on this path. Spiritual traditions, including Christianity, are full of practices that show us how to respond to the compassion planted within us. From the ancient Desert Prayer to the Compassion Practice of today, Christian compassion-forming exercises, processes, and approaches have given us guidance for the way ahead. They have shown us how to follow the threefold call to love defined by Jesus: grounding ourselves in the love of God, loving ourselves, and loving others. And through these practices, across the ages, we receive a boundless invitation—an invitation to turn our entire beings again and again to the spiritual path that Jesus taught, the way of living compassion.

NOTES

Longing for Compassion

1. Frank Rogers, in private conversation.
2. For similar perspectives, see Oliver Davies, *A Theology of Compassion: Metaphysics of Difference and the Renewal of Tradition* (Grand Rapids: Wm. B. Eerdmans Publishing, 2003, especially 16-23; Paul Gilbert, *The Compassionate Mind: A New Approach to Life's Challenges.* (Oakland, CA: New Harbinger Publications, 2010); *Compassion—Bridging Practice and Science*, edited by Tania Singer and Matthias Bolz, accessed September 15, 2106, http://www.compassion-training.org/en/online/index.html, #178, 179.
3. *The Compassionate Instinct: The Science of Human Goodness*, edited by Dacher Keltner, Jason Marsh, and Jeremy Adam Smith (New York: W.W. Norton & Company, 2010). Examples of university-based research and formation programs: http://www.compassion-training.org/—connected with Tania Singer, Max Planck Institute, University of Leipzig; The Greater Good Science Center, University of California, Berkeley, https://greatergood.berkeley.edu /compassion; Center for Healthy Minds, https://centerhealthyminds.org/, University of Wisconsin, Madison.
4. Such practices are often popularly known—sometimes a bit inaccurately—as *Metta*, Loving-Kindness Meditation, Tonglen, and Compassion Meditation.

Chapter 1: Becoming Compassion

1. Compassion definitions are from https://greatergood.berkeley.edu/compassion /definition#what_is, accessed September 15, 2016.
2. http://greatergood.berkeley.edu/topic/compassion/definition#what_is, accessed September 15, 2016. According to some scholar-practitioners, this definition matches some Tibetan Buddhist understandings that separate the terms "compassion" (the desire that someone not suffer), "loving-kindness" (the desire, leading to action, that someone be happy), and bodhicitta (acting to help another be happy). For one version of this, see the Dalai Lama's book *An Open Heart: Practicing Compassion in Everyday Life* (New York: Back Bay Books, 2001) 91, 96, 119. Buddhist scholar John Dunne alludes to these differences between terms in his privately-circulated, unpublished paper, "Compassion in Tibetan Buddhist Practice." Some scholars maintain that this perspective was embraced in the scientific community because, in part, many of the neuroscientists, including neuropsychologists, studying compassion-forming contemplative practices drew their understandings of compassion from their own practice traditions, which were Buddhist-based. For additional, influential perspectives

on these concepts in relation to the nature of emotions, see Olga Klimecki, Matthieu Ricard, and Tania Singer, *Compassion—Bridging Practice and Science*, accessed September 15, 2016, http://www.compassion-training.org/en /online/index.html, #274, and http://www.compassion-training.org/en/online /index.html, #284, and http://www.compassion-training.org/en/online/index .html, #178.

3. The Hebrew words most often translated as "compassion"—and rooted in a sense of the physical churning of the womb or gut—are variations on *rachum*, while the Greek words are variations on *splagchnizomai*. These terms, as well as the Greek words *eleeo*, *oikteiro*, have often been translated into English as "mercy" and "pity," as well as "compassion," and in much of the spiritual writings of the Christian spiritual traditions, mercy, pity, and compassion have been used interchangeably. (See Sara McNamer, *Affective Meditation and the Invention of Medieval Compassion* [Philadelphia: University of Pennsylvania Press, 2010], 11;. also, Oliver Davies, *A Theology of Compassion* Eugene, OR: WiFP and Stock Publishers, 2013]). The biblical texts, if fact, contain no obvious internal principles for not translating these words as "compassion" in every instance of their usage. So an English word that means one thing in, say, seventeenth-century England may mean something quite different in twenty-first-century North America. For example, "deface" once meant "outshine" rather than "vandalize." To complicate things further, centuries before there were English translations of the Bible, the Hebrew and Greek words for compassion were translated into Latin. Translations, of course, have depended on the era and perspectives of the translators. Over the course of Christian history, issues related to the meanings of these words have been made particularly complex by the fact that the dominant early translations of the Greek and Hebrew biblical texts in the Christian West were in Latin. The earliest English versions of the Bible were built on the Latin texts (as they were used in study and in liturgy), which, due to the subtleties of theological and cultural understandings of the medieval church, tended to nuance the meanings of the words in the direction of "mercy" and "pity." Modern translations—and, in turn, current popular uses and understandings—tend to engage "compassion," "pity," and "mercy" in ways that (arguably) do not necessarily correspond with the meanings of the terms as they are used in the biblical texts.

4. Examples include John Macransky and Brooke Lavelle's "Courage of Care" process (http://courageofcare.org/, accessed June 26, 2017), Kristin Neff's self-compassion work (http://self-compassion.org/, accessed September 15, 2016), and Paul Gilbert's *Mindful Compassion: How the Science of Compassion Can Help You Understand Your Emotions, Live in the Present, and Connect Deeply with Others* (Oakland, CA: New Harbinger Publications, 2014).

5. Classically, the interplay between emotion and wisdom has often been framed in terms of the will and the intellect. For example, see Judith A. Barad, "The Understanding and Experience of Compassion: Aquinas and the Dalai Lama." *Buddhist-Christian Studies*, 27 (2007) 11-29, 16.

6. For "restorative justice" see Howard Zehr and Allan MacRae, *The Big Book of Restorative Justice: Four Classic Justice & Peacebuilding Books in One Volume (Justice and Peacebuilding)*, (New York: Good Books, 2015).

7. See John Main, *Word into Silence: A Manual for Christian Meditation* (Norwich: Canterbury Press, 2007).

8. Neuroscientific studies of contemplative practices have focused predominantly on attention and awareness, with relatively minimal research on other capacities. For example, the capacities of expectations, beliefs, and assumptions are

all vital for setting the tone, direction, and outcome of a practice—spiritual or otherwise. Our exploration of compassion in Christianity will include expectations, beliefs, and assumptions within a broad understanding of intentions.

9. My understanding of the role of intimacy draws much from conversations with the author and creative contemplative Mark Yaconelli and with the social neuroscientist Michael Spezio.

10. Emotion researchers tend to separate "feelings" from "emotions." They use the latter term to refer to spontaneous, neurophysiological, pre-conscious reactions to stimuli, while "feeling" refers to a conscious awareness of the automatic reaction that is an emotion. I am using "feelings," and "emotions" interchangeably, while the Christian traditions tend to use "affections" to refer to the range of complex experiences we normally refer to as feelings and emotions.

11. See the 2015 Disney/Pixar movie "Inside Out" for one version of these new scientific understandings.

12. My discussion of Sevenfold Cause and Effect practice relies especially on an unpublished, privately-circulated paper by the Buddhist scholar John Dunne entitled "Compassion in Tibetan Buddhist Practice." For other versions of this practice, see Miles Neale. "Sevenfold Cause and Effect Instruction," accessed September 15, 2016, http://milesneale.blogspot.com/ and The Dalai Lama, *An Open Heart: Practicing Compassion in Everyday Life* (New York: Back Bay Books, 2001), 120-122.

13. Think of spiritual exercises as analogous to playing scales on the piano. Rather than performing a complete musical piece, scales exercises focus on improving one discrete set of capacities (e.g., finger coordination on the keys) in preparation for the musical performance. Likewise, spiritual exercises focus on particular capacities (e.g., attention) in contrast to the more complex and complete process that is a spiritual practice, which may exercise a multitude of capacities as it unfolds.

Chapter 2: Compassion Practices for Grounding in Divine Presence

1. In fact, freezing is the first of the three reactions. See Joseph LeDoux, "'Run, Hide, Fight' Is Not How Our Brains Work," https://www.nytimes.com/2015/12/20/opinion/sunday/run-hide-fight-is-not-how-our-brains-work.html, accessed September 18, 2016.

2. Alane Daugherty, *From Mindfulness to Heartfulness: A Journey of Transformation through the Science of Embodiment* (Bloomington, IN: Balboa Press, 2014), 35-108.

3. See, for example, https://nccih.nih.gov/health/meditation.

4. There are many conversations, worldwide, around what is gained and lost when meditative practices are separated from their spiritual roots. These conversations are especially robust in relation to the mindfulness-training programs in the U.S. military. Mindfulness and the military may at first seem like an odd fit. But the combination does make sense. Studies show that mindfulness practices provide relief for veterans suffering from PTSD. In addition, men and women preparing for combat are taught these practices in order to hone their awareness, steady their attention, regulate their emotions, and increase their resilience. Meditation seems to help soldiers focus more effectively in battle zones, since it reduces inappropriate, automatic reactivity. This keeps soldiers safe. It also saves other lives. For example, regular mindfulness practice might decrease the chance that soldiers would shoot at a harmless child who happens

to dart out in front of them on a potentially dangerous street. Of course, even as lives are saved, this may raise some moral and ethical issues within the ancient religious traditions that developed mindfulness practices in the first place. For instance, strengthening the ability to focus attention and regulate emotion can help a military sharpshooter take out a human target more easily. Many founders of pacifist traditions behind mindfulness practices might be appalled at the thought of using their spiritual practice to help take a life, whatever the reason. For discussions of this issue see Judd Brewer, "Mindfulness in the Military," *American Journal of Psychiatry* http://ajp.psychiatryonline.org/toc/ajp/171/8, pp. 803-806, accessed September 18, 2016; http://ajp.psychiatryonline.org/doi /abs/10.1176/appi.ajp.2014.14040501; Alena Hall, "How Mindfulness Practices Can Help Prepare Military Members for Future Combat," accessed September 18, 2016, http://www.huffingtonpost.com/2015/03/10/mindfulness-in-the -military_n_6833402.html. I bring this issue up here to emphasize that religious and "secular" perspectives on meditative practices may not necessarily match up. Spiritual traditions may not value the same benefits of the practices that non-religious teachers of the practice may value.

5. The first time I heard Dr. Hanson name this was in a private conversation with him. For more on this topic, see his book *Buddha's Brain: The Practical Neuroscience of Happiness, Love, and Wisdom* (Oakland, CA: New Harbinger Publications, Inc., 2009) for an accessible take on this expanding field.

6. Perhaps a model human love relationship should be experienced in order to experience Divine Presence. But at the very least, the experience of divine Presence seems possible because of our innate relational capacities.

7. Many Psalms and prayers in the Bible and in early Christianity have served to ground Christians in Compassion. But I find no prayer formulas earlier than this one that were specifically designed to be used in the way the desert monastics used their prayer.

8. John Cassian, "Conference 10. The Second Conference of Abbot Isaac. On Prayer," in *Conferences*, Chapter 10. "Continual prayer" refers to the biblical injunction to "pray without ceasing" (1 Thess. 5:17). John Cassian (according to his own report) spent twenty to thirty years (until about 399 CE) with desert hermits in Egypt and Palestine. He wrote the *Conferences* and the *Institutes* from approximately 425 to 430 CE as compilations of what he learned and heard from the desert sages he visited. Benedict of Nursia and many others in western Christianity—including the Celts—read and used Cassian's works as the basis for the monasticism that later arose beyond the desert.

9. Cassian, Ibid.

10. The practice draws on the Jewish and Christian traditions of venerating the name of the Divine, though the former tradition honored God by refraining from speaking God's name, while the latter honored God by invoking the divine name in a way that sought to lift it up as the most cherished of all names. For example, when the Hebrew bible is read aloud, other words for God are substituted for YHWH. And see Philippians 2:10, which asserts that all people will bow in homage when the name of Jesus is spoken. Veneration of divine names also appears in religions other than Christianity, including traditions of Hinduism, Buddhism, and Islam.

11. For a helpful description of "attachment theory," see David Wallin, *Attachment in Psychotherapy* (New York: The Guilford Press, 2007).

12. Teresa of Avila was not your ordinary, run-of-the-mill, sixteenth-century nun. A contemplative activist committed to reforming her religious order, she never ceased to challenge the entrenched church hierarchy of her day. She traveled a

great deal, meeting with bishops, the Pope, and other leaders of her time, constantly urging them to support a return to her order's original vision for itself.

13. Teresa of Avila, *The Interior Castle*. See especially the third chapter of the fourth Dwelling Place.

14. Francis de Sales quotes these last two images in his description of Recollection in *The Treatise on the Love of God*, Book 6, Chapter 7. Here are some of Teresa's descriptions of the practice: "Do you believe, that it is of little importance for a soul who is easily distracted, to understand this truth [that God is in it] and to know that, in order to speak with its heavenly Father and to enjoy His company it does not have to go up to heaven or even to raise its voice? No matter how softly it speaks, He always hears it, because He is so near. It does not need wings to go to contemplate Him in itself. . . .The soul collects together all its faculties and enters within itself to be with its God." Teresa of Avila, *The Way of Perfection*, 28, accessed September 15, 2016, http://sufferingwith joy.com/2012/04/21/the-prayer-of-recollection/; http://carmelnet.org/larkin /larkin083.pdf, 397, accessed September 15, 2016; https://archive.org/stream/teresas ownwords00tereuoft/teresasownwords00tereuoft_djvu.txt, accessed September 15, 2016.

15. Dwight H. Judy, *Embracing God: Praying with Teresa of Avila* (Nashville: Abingdon Press, 1996), 80-81.

16. Teresa of Avila, *The Way of Perfection*, Chapter 29.

17. Teresa of Avila, *The Way of Perfection*, Chapter 26.

18. Teresa of Avila, *The Way of Perfection*, Chapter 29.

19. Teresa of Avila, *The Way of Perfection*, Chapter 26.

20. Pennington references Galatians 5:22-23 in listing the "fruits of the Spirit" as "love, joy, peace, patience, kindness, benignity, gentleness, long-suffering, and chastity." Basil Pennington, *Centering Prayer: Renewing an Ancient Christian Prayer Form* (New York: Doubleday, 2001), 121.

21. See Thomas Keating, *Intimacy with God* (New York: Crossroad, 1994), 11–21; Thomas Keating, *Manifesting God* (New York: Lantern Books, 2005), 118–23; Thomas Keating, *Open Mind, Open Heart: The Contemplative Dimension of the Gospel* (Warwick, NY: Amity House, 1986), 143; Basil Pennington, *Centering Prayer: Renewing an Ancient Christian Prayer Form* (New York: Doubleday, 2001), 55; Basil Pennington, "Introduction," in *Centering Prayer in Daily Life and Ministry*, ed. Gustave Reininger (New York: Continuum, 1998), 10; Gustave Reininger, "The Christian Contemplative Tradition and Centering Prayer," in *Centering Prayer in Daily Life and Ministry*, ed. Gustave Reininger (New York: Continuum, 1998), 26.

22. Keating, *Intimacy with God*, 13.

23. Keating, *Intimacy with God*, 15.

24. Quoted in Carl J. Arico, *A Taste of Silence: Centering Prayer and the Contemplative Journey* (New York: Continuum, 1999), 144. Basil Pennington makes a similar point in paraphrasing a section of Chapter 3 of the medieval spiritual writing *The Cloud of Unknowing*: "Center all your attention and desire on him and let this be the sole concern of your mind and heart." See Pennington, *Centering Prayer: Renewing an Ancient Christian Prayer Form*, 26. References to *The Cloud* will appear again and again in our examination of Centering Prayer. It is important to note that although those who formed Centering Prayer took *The Cloud of Unknowing* as their primary inspiration, for our study it is not important to understand what *The Cloud* expresses, but rather to understand what Centering Prayer practitioners say about how they use *The Cloud* (or any other historical writings) to inform the theory and practice of Centering

Prayer. Teachers of Centering Prayer both ground their perspective in ancient thought and consciously, intentionally deviate from it as they see fit. Their use of *The Cloud* reflects that practice. For example, though *The Cloud* exhibits the dominant medieval, western model of human nature (a body and soul construction, with the soul consisting of mind, reason, and will), those who developed Centering Prayer lean heavily upon twentieth-century western psychology for their anthropology. At the same time, Keating sometimes uses the medieval terminology (without embracing its entire meaning) found in *The Cloud* when describing human nature. For example, he characterizes the human being as comprised of a body (the physical dimension), a soul (which contains the emotions), and spirit (the place of God's presence and action and the dimension directly addressed by Centering Prayer). Keating, *Intimacy with God*, 101–2. For a description of the model of human nature underlying *The Cloud*, see Phyllis Hodgson, "Introduction to the Cloud of Unknowing," in *The Cloud of Unknowing and Related Treatises*, Analecta Cartusiana (Salzburg, Austria: Institut für Anglistik und Amerikanistik, Universität Salzburg, 1982), xxxv–xli. Consistent with Christian contemplative practices throughout the ages, the practice was seen not as contemplation itself (which is a divine gift not subject to human effort), but as "a preparation for contemplation." Keating, *Intimacy with God*, 11.

25. Carl Arico, *A Taste of Silence*, 144, notes that this use of "centered" appears in a letter Merton wrote to the Sufi scholar Abdul Aziz: "Simply speaking, I have a very simple way of prayer. It is centered entirely on the presence of God and to His will and His love. That is to say, it is centered on Faith by which alone we can know the presence of God. One might say this gives my meditation the character described by the Prophet (Mohammad) as being before God as if you saw him. Yet it does not mean imagining anything or conceiving a precious image of God. To my mind, this would be a form of idolatry. On the contrary it is a manner of adoring Him as all." Arico is quoting (without citing a page number) from *Thomas Merton, Brother Monk* by Basil Pennington.

26. Cynthia Bourgeault emphasizes "consent" and "availability" in her *Centering Prayer and Inner Awakening* (Lanham, MD: Cowley Publications, 2004), 22.

27. These instructions appear within the four-step set of guidelines in Keating, *Manifesting God*, 133–36.

28. This care included attention to how the similar use of words or phrases has appeared throughout the history of the Christian contemplative tradition. Once again, *The Cloud of Unknowing* served as a formative source, as Carl Arico points out in quoting a pertinent section from Chapter 7: "This word should be your defense in conflict and in peace. Use it to beat upon the cloud of darkness about you. Subdue all distractions, consigning them to a cloud of forgetting beneath you. . . . It is best when this word is wholly interior without a definite thought or actual sound. . . . [I]ts value lies in its simplicity." It is worth noting that where most versions of *The Cloud* use "thoughts," Arico uses "distractions." See Arico, 140–41. The developers of the prayer also identify other sources from the tradition that similarly use a word or phrase, particularly Abba Isaac's seventh-century instructions to pray using Psalm verses. See, for example, Pennington, *Centering Prayer*, 17.

29. Basil Pennington quotes Chapter 7 of *The Cloud of Unknowing* as a formative influence in this understanding of the form and nature of the word: "If you want to gather all you desire into one simple word that the mind can easily retain, choose a short word, rather than a long one, a single syllable is best, like *God* or *love*," and "If your mind begins to intellectualize over the meaning and

connotations of this little word, remind yourself that its value lies in its simplicity." Pennington, *Centering Prayer*, 26–27.

30. Ibid.
31. Keating, *Intimacy with God*, 68.
32. "The sacred word is an intention, a movement of the will toward the spiritual level of our being": Keating, *Intimacy with God*, 99. Thus, as no more and no less than a catalyzing "gesture or sign of accepting God as He is," the "word" may simply be "an inward glance toward God" or "noticing our breathing as a symbol of the Spirit." Keating, *Open Mind, Open Heart: The Contemplative Dimension of the Gospel*, 50. See also, Keating, *Manifesting God*, 107. Others who practice the prayer have noted that a simple motion, a sound, or image can substitute for the word. Its purpose is to be a reminder to return to your intention, nothing more.
33. Keating, *Open Mind, Open Heart: The Contemplative Dimension of the Gospel*, 36.
34. Think of the (unfortunately, often-parodied) repetition of the sacred sound of *om*. John Main's version of Christian meditation is a mantric practice of this type and is, in fact, drawn from Hindu practices. Main substitutes *maranatha* for *om*. John Main, *Word into Silence: A Manual for Christian Meditation* (Norwich: Canterbury Press, 2007).
35. Bourgeault, *Centering Prayer and Inner Awakening*, 23–24.
36. Keating, *Manifesting God*, 94–95.
37. Keating, *Manifesting God*, 83, 95–96.
38. Keating, *Manifesting God*, 133–36. While a handful of different versions of the prayer exist, this one—as taught by Father Keating and the Centering Prayer organization, Contemplative Outreach—has become the most widely practiced. Contemplative Outreach was formed in 1983-84 by a group of monastics, clergy, and lay persons committed to Christian transformation especially grounded in the practice of Centering Prayer. Descriptions of the history and development of Contemplative Outreach can be found at http://www.contemplativeoutreach.org/history-centering-prayer (accessed September 15, 2016) and in Keating, *Intimacy with God*, 19–21.
39. Pennington, *Centering Prayer*, xv-xvi.
40. This practice comes from exercises connected to the Compassion Practice as described in Frank Rogers, *Practicing Compassion* (Nashville: Fresh Air Books, 2015).

Chapter 3: Compassion Practices for Yourself

1. The Jesus Prayer seems to have grown out of the tradition of the Prayer of the Desert. For reasons that are lost to history, the mantric use of Psalm verses to invoke compassion faded. Biblical phrases were still repeated, but now they came from the gospels and centered on the name of Jesus rather than on naming God. I am using one of the most common versions of the prayer. Other versions are longer, ending with "have compassion on me, a sinner." The Greek word *eleison* translated here as "compassion" is one of the cluster of terms also translated as "mercy" and "pity." The biblical texts from which this prayer is drawn describe requests for Jesus to heal and usually translate the Greek word as "mercy" (Mark 10: 47-48; Matthew 20:30-31; Luke 18:38-39). In these passages the request for mercy/compassion comes from blind men. In the worldview of biblical times such a disability was seen as being a result of human sinfulness or unworthiness. So to ask for mercy was to ask for forgiveness and

the freedom from suffering that comes with that sense of release in feeling for-
given. Later theological treatments of the Latin word *misericordia* translated
as "mercy" define it in ways that are synonymous with understandings of the
Latin term *compassio* (compassion). For this latter point in relation to Thomas
Aquinas, see Judith A. Barad, "The Understanding and Experience of Compassion: Aquinas and the Dalai Lama," *Buddhist-Christian Studies*, 27 (2007), 12.
These days, most scholars agree that "compassion" most accurately captures
the contemporary meaning of the ancient Greek, Latin, and Hebrew terms that
have also been translated—without consistency or logic—as mercy and pity.

2. This paragraph's description (including quotes) of the three parts of human
beings and the Jesus prayer comes from Timothy Ware, "Introduction," *The
Art of Prayer: An Orthodox Anthology*, compiled by Igumen Chariton of Valamo, translated by E. Kadloubovsky and E. M. Palmer (London: Faber, 1966),
17-18. Teachers in the tradition name these three dimensions in various ways.
For instance, some teachers refer to mind as "soul," while others refer to it as
"intellect." And sometimes "spirit" is used in place of heart.

3. The general flow of the following summary of the three "degrees" of the Jesus
Prayer is drawn especially from Timothy Ware, "Introduction," *The Art of
Prayer*, 21-23.

4. "[I]t is not the act of repetition itself . . . but *to whom* we speak that imbues
the prayer with its power": (Kallistos Ware, *The Power of the Name: The Jesus
Prayer in Orthodox Spirituality*, Fairacres Publication (Oxford: SLG Press,
1986), 23.

5. Calistus and Ignatius of Xanthopoulos, "Direction to Hesychasts," *Writings
from the Philokalia on Prayer of the Heart*, translated and edited by E. Kadloubovsky and G. E. H. Palmer (London: Faber & Faber, 1951), 239, #73. Calistus and Ignatius refer here to this process of pondering over the words as "an
inner movement of the heart," which points to a certain artificiality in a strict
separation between the three movements of the Jesus Prayer.

6. Ibid.

7. Greek: *mnimi*, which is translated as "remembrance" or "mindfulness."

8. Timothy Ware, "Introduction," *The Art of Prayer*, 28.

9. While Theophan the Recluse identifies these three broad movements, he also
calls the prayer of the mind *effort-filled* "prayer of the heart," while the third
level is *effortless* "prayer of the heart." Igumen Chariton of Valamo, et al., *The
Art of Prayer*, 63–66.

10. Igumen Chariton of Valamo, et al., *The Art of Prayer*, 67, and Gregory of
Sinai, "On Prayer: Seven Texts," #4, in *The Philokalia: The Complete Text*,
vol. 4, compiled by St. Nikodimos of the Holy Mountain and St. Makarios of
Corinth, translated and edited by G. E. H. Palmer, Phillip Sherrard, and Kallistos Ware (London: Faber & Faber, 1995), 277.

11. Timothy Ware, "Introduction," *The Art of Prayer*, 26, quoting Theophan the
Recluse. Theophan also describes the experience in this way: "[T]he convic-
tion . . . that God is in you, as He is in everything . . . must not be accompanied
by any visual concept, but must be confined to a simple . . . feeling. A man in
a warm room feels how the warmth envelops and penetrates him. The same
must be the effect on our spiritual nature of the . . . presence of God, who is
the fire in the room of our being." Igumen Chariton of Valamo, et al., *The Art
of Prayer*, 100. Isaac of Nineveh (7th century, CE) pointed to the importance
of feeling emotions in prayer when he wrote that when a monk is praying he
may "sometimes . . . add feeling to the words and repeat them slowly. On occasion the feeling . . . will cause all sorts of deeply-felt words of prayer; or joy

may burst forth . . . , stirring that person to alter his prayer to praises. . . ." See
Isaac of Nineveh, "Texts on Prayer and Outward Posture during Prayer," *The Syriac Fathers on Prayer and the Spiritual Life*, translated by Sebastian Brock (Kalamazoo: Cistercian Publications, 1987), 290.

12. Timothy Ware, "Introduction," *The Art of Prayer*, 26, quoting Theophan the Recluse.

13. Isaac of Nineveh, "On Pure Prayer," in *The Syriac Fathers on Prayer and the Spiritual Life*, ed. and trans. Sebastian Brock (Kalamazoo, Mich.: Cistercian Publications, 1987), 293.

14. Nicholas E. Lombardo, *The Logic of Desire: Aquinas on Emotion* (Washington, D.C.: Catholic University of America Press, 2011), 118, 122, 125.

15. For example, according to Isaac of Nineveh (7th century, CE), "After many years of struggle the advanced sweep away all imagination, both proper and improper, so that no trace of it remains." "On Pure Prayer," in *The Syriac Fathers on Prayer and the Spiritual Life*, ed. and trans. Sebastian Brock (Kalamazoo, Mich.: Cistercian Publications, 1987), 297. This rare state appears to be what some writers call ecstasy (*ekstasis*). Gregory of Sinai (14th century, CE) wrote that *ekstasis* involves "not only the heavenward ravishing of the soul's power; it is also complete transcendence of the sense-world itself." Gregory of Sinai, "On Commandments and Doctrines," #58, *The Philokalia: The Complete Text*, vol. 4. Compiled by St. Nikodimos of the Holy Mountain and St. Makarios of Corinth, translated and edited by G. E. H. Palmer, Phillip Sherrard, and Kallistos Ware (London: Faber & Faber, 1995), 222.

Chapter 4: Compassion Practices for Others

1. Frank Rogers Jr., *Compassion in Practice: The Way of Jesus* (Nashville: Upper Room Books, 2016), 93-94. For the sake of clarity in the context of my reason for relating Frank's experience, this is an edited and condensed version of the original, which is part of a larger story that is well worth reading in its entirety.

2. Frank Rogers, Jr., *Compassion in Practice: The Way of Jesus*, 94.

3. In Latin: *Meditationes vitae Christi*. The works I'm referring to as the *Meditations* began showing up in the twelfth century and continued appearing into the fifteenth century. While their titles were not always "Meditations on the Life of Christ," they show a style and a purpose like that of the most popular version, which appeared in the thirteenth century. Denise N. Baker, "The Privity of the Passion," *Cultures of Piety: Medieval English Devotional Literature in Translation*, edited by Anne Clark Bartlett and Thomas H. Bestul (Ithaca: Cornell University Press, 1999), 85-86. I use several of these texts to explore the formation of compassion for others.

4. You may remember that the imagination is engaged in Teresa of Avila's practice of Recollection when she asks us to picture Jesus on the cross. Teresa's focus on imagination makes sense since her tradition has roots in the practices of the *Meditations*. But unlike Teresa and the writers of the *Meditations*, teachers of Desert Prayer, the Jesus Prayer, and the Cloud of Unknowing/Centering Prayer practices found that using the imagination is counterproductive for many people; it draws attention away from God and onto fantasies, daydreaming, or worse. So the practice traditions avoided imagination, focused on sacred words, encouraged feelings of Divine Presence, and cultivated God-ward intention rather than on creations of the imagination.

5. Sarah McNamer calls them "'intimate scripts' . . . for the performance of feeling." Sarah McNamer, *Affective Meditation and the Invention of Medieval Compassion* (Philadelphia: University of Pennsylvania Press, 2010), 12.

6. ". . . The text urges the reader to *envisage* the events of Christ's life; the mind and the heart are themselves endowed with eyes, and of all the senses it is vision that apprehends its object most vividly and immediately. The *Meditationes* further induce vivid imagination by rhetorical devices, by inviting the reader to join imaginatively in solving problems (what to do, for example, about removing the body from the cross?), and by posing questions about the course of events." Richard Kieckhefer, "Recent Work on Pseudo-Bonaventure and Nicholas Love," *Mystics Quarterly* 21, no. 2 (1995): 44, accessed September 18, 2016. http://www.jstor.org.dtl.idm.oclc.org/stable/20717242.

These steps are part of a broader process common to this tradition of meditations. Elizabeth Salter identifies this process as consisting of a detailed, realistic "description of a scene or event"; "emotional reflection" on what the pray-er is or should be experiencing affectively in relation to this scene; and a description of the "moral application" of this experience in the pray-er's life. Elizabeth Salter, *Nicholas Love's "Myrrour of the Blessed Lyf of Jesu Christ,"* vol. 10 of *Analecta Cartusiana*, edited by James Hogg (Salzburg: Institut Für Englische Sprache und Literatur, 1974), 158. Salter's perspective is noted and expanded by Denise Despres, *Ghostly Sights: Visual Meditation in Late-Medieval Literature* (Norman, Oklahoma: Pilgrim Books, 1989), 6-7.

7. Denise N. Baker, "The Privity of the Passion," *Cultures of Piety: Medieval English Devotional Literature in Translation*, edited by Anne Clark Bartlett and Thomas H. Bestul (Ithaca: Cornell University Press, 1999. 85-106), 90-91.

8. Nicholas Love, *The Mirror of the Blessed Life of Jesu Christ*, edited by a Monk of Parkminster (London: Burns, Oates, and Washbourne, 1926), XLII, 227.

9. Love, XLIV, 237.

10. Love, XLIV, 237. Sarah McNamer argues that in asking readers to identify with Mary, the *Mirror* and similar texts present compassion as a particularly female response, rather than a broadly human response, and invites male readers to become female in this regard. For this perspective and for the source of my more general point that readers are being invited to live into the compassionate feelings of Jesus' mother, see Sarah McNamer, *Affective Meditation and the Invention of Medieval Compassion*. Also see Elizabeth Salter, *Nicholas Love's "Myrrour of the Blessed Lyf of Jesu Christ."* vol. 10 of *Analecta Cartusiana*, edited by James Hogg (Salzburg: Institut Für Englische Sprache und Literatur,1974), 133-142.

11. Love, XLIV, 237.

12. Denise N. Baker, "The Privity of the Passion," 94. See also: "[His mother] hung in soul with her Son upon the cross." Love, XLIII, 234.

13. Love, XLIII, 237.

14. Dan Merkur, *Crucified with Christ: Meditation on the Passion, Mystical Death, and the Medieval Invention of Psychotherapy* (Syracuse: State University of New York Press, 2008), 2-6.

15. Walter Hilton, *The Goad of Love: an unpublished translation of the* Stimulus Amoris *formerly attributed to St. Bonaventura*, edited by Clare Kirchberger (London: Faber and Faber, Ltd., 1952), ch 4, 70. Hilton lists this as the fifth of six steps in a process of imagining oneself into Jesus' passion and compassion. These six steps are elaborated somewhat differently in chapter 4 of *Stimuli Divini Amoris*, a 1642 English translation (of a Vatican-approved version) of

Stimuli Amoris revised and edited by W. A. Phillipson (London: R. & T. Washbourne, LTD: 1907).

16. Walter Hilton, *The Goad of Love*, ch 4, 70.
17. *Stimuli Divini Amoris, The Goad of Divine Love,* a 1642 English translation revised and edited by W. A. Phillipson (London: R. & T. Washbourne, LTD, 1907), ch 4, 34.
18. Hilton describes seven "works of mercy and of pity" derived from Matthew 25, in particular: feeding the hungry, housing the homeless, clothing the naked, visiting the sick and the imprisoned, and burying the dead: Walter Hilton, *The Goad of Love*, 92. The versions of *The Goad* make no clear, consistent distinctions between the meanings of mercy, pity, and compassion; all three terms function interchangeably. For consistency, I am using "compassion" when the text of the *Meditations* uses "mercy" and "pity."
19. Walter Hilton, *The Goad of Love*, 94-95.
20. For background on the "Spiritual Exercises of St. Ignatius," I recommend the following: Javier Melloni, *The Exercises in the Western Tradition* (Herefordshire: Gracewing, 2000); Katherine Marie Dyckman, Mary Garvin, Elizabeth Liebert, *The Spiritual Exercises Reclaimed: Uncovering Liberating Possibilities for Women* (Mahwah, NJ: Paulist Press, 2001).
21. Kenneth L. Becker, *Unlikely Companions: C. G. Jung on the Spiritual Exercises of Ignatius of Loyola,* (Leominster, England: Gracewing, 2002).
22. I thank Jeremy Bakker for the summary ideas in this paragraph and the one that follows.

Chapter 5: A Compassion Practice for Our Time

1. Many traditions of psychology have versions of this understanding as well, with these "movements" being known by a variety of names and viewed as having positive, negative, or neutral impacts on human wellbeing.
2. For a brilliant description of how this works, see Bessel van der Kolk, *The Body Keeps the Score: Brain, Mind, and Body in the Healing of Trauma* (New York: Viking, 2014).
3. I admit that to make a point I am giving the most simplistic example possible. This practice contains characteristics common to many practices, but I do not mean to attach it to any particular practice tradition.
4. *The Rule of St Benedict of Nursia*, "Prologue," verse 28.
5. Nicholas E. Lombardo, *The Logic of Desire: Aquinas on Emotion* (Washington, D.C.: Catholic University of America Press, 2011), 118, 122, 125. Aquinas's view shows up strongly in Ignatius and the Franciscans.
6. Expanded versions of Frank's teaching on that day eventually showed up in his books *Practicing Compassion* and *Compassion in Practice: The Way of Jesus.*
7. The Compassion Practice is not the only spiritual or therapeutic process that carries this perspective. Others include Nonviolent Communication, Internal Family Systems, and Focusing. See Marshal Rosenberg, *Living Nonviolent Communication: Practical Tools to Connect and Communicate Skillfully in Every Situation* (Boulder: Sounds True, 2012); Richard Schwartz, *Introduction to the Internal Family Systems Model* (Oak Park, IL: Trailheads Publications, 2001); Ann Weiser Cornell, *The Power of Focusing: A Practical Guide to Emotional Self-Healing* (Oakland, CA: New Harbinger Press, 1996).
8. To extend this metaphor, we could think of this process as semaphore, the communication technique of waving flags to convey messages at a distance. The

maritime world adopted and widely used semaphores (with hand-held flags replacing the mechanical arms of shutter semaphores) in the 19th century.

9. *The Compassionate Instinct: The Science of Human Goodness,* edited by Dacher Keltner, Jason Marsh, and Jeremy Adam Smith (New York: W. W Norton & Company, 2010), 6.

10. http://www.contemplativemind.org/practices/tree/loving-kindness, accessed September 18, 2016. The Dalai Lama, *An Open Heart: Practicing Compassion in Everyday Life* (New York: Back Bay Books, 2001), 120-122.

11. The fact that different processes work for different people is a very good indication of the need for variety in practices.

12. Olga Klimecki, Matthieu Ricard, and Tania Singer note how empathy and compassion differ in neural processes and experience. Empathy is simply sharing the experience of the other, so can lead to burnout, while compassion is "a warm positive state associated with a strong prosocial motivation" that furthers resilience. Olga Klimecki, Matthieu Ricard, and Tania Singer, "Empathy versus Compassion," *Compassion—Bridging Practice and Science,* accessed September 19, 2016, http://www.compassion-training.org/en/online/index.html?ifra me=true&width=100%&height=100%#274, http://www.compassion-training .org/en/online/index.html?iframe=true&width=100%&height=100%#284.

13. Here I'll offer only a broad overview. For the complete details of the practice, see Frank Rogers, Jr., *Compassion in Practice: The Way of Jesus* (Nashville: Upper Room Books, 2016) and *Practicing Compassion* (Nashville: Fresh Air Books, 2015). All the exercises, practices, and processes described here are drawn from these two books and from the courses, retreats, curricula, and programs of training and formation related to the Compassion Practice, as developed by the Center for Engaged Compassion (www.centerforengagedcompassion.com).

For those who hunger for deep spiritual experience . . .

The Academy for Spiritual Formation® is an experience of disciplined Christian community emphasizing holistic spirituality—nurturing body, mind, and spirit. The program, a ministry of The Upper Room®, is ecumenical in nature and meant for all those who hunger for a deeper relationship with God, including both lay and clergy. Each Academy fosters spiritual rhythms—of study and prayer, silence and liturgy, solitude and relationship, rest and exercise. With offerings of both Two-Year and Five-Day models, Academy participants rediscover Christianity's rich spiritual heritage through worship, learning, and fellowship. The Academy's commitment to an authentic spirituality promotes balance, inner and outer peace, holy living and justice living—God's shalom.

Faculty trained in the wide breadth of Christian spirituality and practice provide content and guidance at each session of The Academy. Academy faculty presenters come from seminaries, monasteries, spiritual direction ministries, and pastoral ministries or other settings and are from a variety of traditions.

The Academy Recommends program seeks to highlight content that aligns with the Academy's mission to provide resources and settings where pilgrims encounter the teachings, sustaining practices, and rhythms that foster attentiveness to God's Spirit and therefore help spiritual leaders embody Christ's presence in the world.

Learn more here: http://academy.upperroom.org/.

CPSIA information can be obtained
at www.ICGtesting.com
Printed in the USA
FSOW02n1716130218
44515FS